Sexual Divide

A Journey of Hope to Bridge the Chasm

by

George L. Olson

authorHOUSE™

1663 LIBERTY DRIVE, SUITE 200
BLOOMINGTON, INDIANA 47403
(800) 839-8640
WWW.AUTHORHOUSE.COM

First published by AuthorHouse 02/01/05

ISBN: 1-4208-1602-0 (sc)

Printed in the United States of America
Bloomington, Indiana

This book is printed on acid-free paper.

Acknowledgments

A number of people helped me in writing this book. Special thanks go to Libby Grandy and the Writers' Critique Group at Borders in Montclair, California, and to Miriam, my wife, who offered critical suggestions and helped with proofreading.

Table of Contents

Author's Note

No problem provokes as strong a controversy in the Lutheran Church as that of homosexual practices. As far as I know, no author has attempted to sort out the issues in a story format. Primarily to help me clarify the problems, I chose to write *Sexual Divide*.

Because church bodies are in a race against time, I have set the issues in a fictional Lutheran Church called Concordia Lutheran Church, USA. To non-Lutherans unfamiliar with the Lutheran Reformation of the 16th century, using *Concordia* in the name can be confusing. It is not limited to the Lutheran Church-Missouri Synod which operates Concordia Theological Seminary in St. Louis. There are several Concordia colleges, both in the LC-MS and the Evangelical Lutheran Church in America, ELCA.

The use of *Concordia* dates back to the post-Reformation era when the various Lutheran churches on the European continent sought to systematize Lutheran teachings in a way that would bring concord (harmony) to all Lutheran churches. By naming my fictional Lutheran church Concordia, I am aiming to further concord among all Lutherans.

Although I aim primarily at Lutherans, Christians of other communions will be able to identify with the characters in *Sexual Divide, A Journey of Hope to Bridge the Chasm*.

May you struggle with the issues and find your way through to a God-pleasing resolution.

George L. Olson, August 25, 2004

1

"Listen to Me"

After Joe Weaver's miraculous golf victory in the Southern California Open, he faded out of sight. He excused his passivity by daily repeating a phrase from his prayer book: "I thank thee that my work ends and thy work begins." He let his golf mantra "Yes, let it be," become an excuse for withdrawing from activities.

All that changed in January, 2004, when he received an invitation to be a delegate to the convention of the Concordia Lutheran Church-USA's Southern California Synod. Joe had always kept his name off the candidate list because he hated to drive long distances on crowded freeways. But since this year it would be held at the Red Roof Inn in Ontario, that would mean only a 20-minute commute from home. The hot item on the agenda was to be sexuality. That topic intrigued him. He wanted to learn more.

On Saturday morning as he read the closing words of the confession, his body suddenly began to quiver. It felt like someone trying to wake him. Anita, his wife, was nowhere in sight. Then a still small voice whispered in his ear, "Wake up! You've avoided the fray long enough. Put your name up for election. You have no excuse for not attending this year."

"But, Lord," he protested. "I've been away from church politics too long."

"Be still. Listen to me," the voice said. "Fill out the application. Send it in today."

Within minutes, Joe had filled out the form, stuck it in the envelope and fastened it with a clothespin to the mailbox. Returning to his recliner in the living room, he wondered how in the world the Southern California Synod would handle the debate over whether or not the national church should approve the blessing of same-sex couples and the ordaining of non-celibate homosexuals. Coming from Japan, where the churches never discussed this issue, Joe needed to study the various views. As an outsider and out of the loop in U.S. church affairs, he realized he might be able to bring a fresh perspective to the debate. He had no personal ax to grind and was beholden to no one — except to his wife Anita. She had directed a telephone counseling service in Tokyo. Her expertise in non-judgmental listening predisposed her to sympathize with gays and lesbians who often were frightened by the prevalent antipathy toward their life style. Joe, on the other hand, felt concerned about the increased toleration of non-traditional family patterns.

In mid-January, four months before the local Synod's convention, Joe decided to attend a meeting of the Mt. Baldy Conference pastors. It was billed as a warm-up for the convention. But before then, the issue became personalized in the dilemma a young seminary intern faced. Like for most Protestant ministerial students, the tradition almost dictated that before ordination he would need to find a suitable woman to marry. Dating back to Martin Luther's marriage to the ex-nun, Katarina Von Bora, the Protestant churches prided themselves in exhibiting model marriages and wholesome family life. Joe felt uneasy about how homosexuals were being shown in a favorable light by movies and television.

The sexuality problem was driven home to Joe during the coffee hour at Grace Alone Lutheran Church. The church's minister, Aaron Blomberg, on the Sunday after Epiphany, preached a powerful sermon on how the congregation must be a welcoming community. He said that no matter how society judged the biblical character of Zachaeus, the tax collector, and Mary Magdalene, the prostitute,

Jesus welcomed them into his inner circle and ate with them. We should, too.

After worship, Joe hurried to the head of the refreshment line to grab a cup of coffee and a cookie. Because he habitually talked with his hands, he sat on the bench next to a table where he could set his cup, relishing his drink with no fear of spilling.

He noticed that Bill Scully, the student from the Theological Seminary of the West (TSW), did not join the coffee line. *That's strange, a student who didn't want any free refreshments.* Their eyes met as Bill approached.

"Do you mind if I join you?" he asked.

"No coffee or juice today?" Joe asked.

"I'm okay. Would you mind if I talked with you in private?"

"No problem. Why don't we move into the fireside room?"

Avoiding other people, the two entered the fellowship building and took seats across from each other in front of the television set.

"Is this okay? I don't think anyone will bother us here. Well, what's on your mind?"

"I apologize for troubling you, but I just can't talk to my advisor at the seminary, Michael McGibbon. I can't tell him about my problem. He's too involved on the gay-rights side of things."

"So, you thought you'd be safe with this old geezer, eh?"

Bill smiled. "You don't seem too old, but you're sort of free aren't you? You're not part of the church or seminary establishment. I think you can be more fair by not being bound by any organization. Does that make sense?"

"If you say so. I'm on the shelf since retiring from overseas."

Bill's eyes twitched as he started to explain himself. "I'm in my last year before graduation. For nine months I've been going with a girl at the sem. Her name is Sally Ryan. We get along fine, but she's more like a sister than a sweetheart."

"So, what's bothering you?"

"I'm more drawn to guys than to girls. You see my problem. If I'm openly gay, they'll never ordain me. I'm Lutheran. That's my church. I could go over to the UCC and get ordained, but I want to stay in the church I've grown up in."

3

"I don't have any pat answer," Joe replied as he shook his head. "Our whole denomination is struggling over your issue. It may split the church. Maybe you can help me, too. I don't have any solution yet — at least one I'm confident the whole church would buy into."

Joe glanced at his watch. "Oh, I've got to run. Lunch is 12:30 at Eternally Young Retirement Center. Why don't we pray and continue this conversation next Sunday if you can wait that long?" He reached over and placed a hand on Bill's folded hands.

"Dear Lord and Savior, help Bill, help me as we grope after truth and your way of love. Amen."

Opening their eyes, Bill and Joe sat quietly, neither speaking another word. Finally Joe broke the spell. "Give me a call. We need to talk more."

He stood up, but Bill remained seated, looking away at nothing in particular. "Yes," he said, "I'll call you at home."

Joe began to walk away, but Bill showed no sign of moving.

2
The Warm-up

Monday morning Joe attended the Mt. Baldy ministerial meeting. He rode with Pastor Blomberg to Bethany Church in Ontario where the meeting would be held. The local dean, Pastor Henry Johnson of Rialto, had included retired ministers in his invitation. "We need all the wisdom we can muster," he said.

He repeated those same words as he called the meeting to order. Immediately Pastor Erik Saulgren, an old joker from Rancho Cucamonga, blurted out, "Then what are all these young ministers doing here?"

Young David Hansen quipped back, "To keep you old guys serious." It was meant to be humorous, but Joe realized it was more than that. The older ministers needed to realize how important sexuality issues were becoming. The young men had trouble even discussing it with parishioners.

Pastor Gonzales of St. Luke's in Yucaipa spoke up. "Several Sundays ago, after the general prayer, I asked the congregants to offer their own intercessions. We were shocked when an older man, who wasn't a member, boomed out a prayer that all homosexuals should repent. Fortunately the woman chair of our church council countered with her own prayer for God to help everyone feel welcome in God's house. We almost had a blowout after church, but over cookies and coffee the storm eventually calmed down."

Dean Johnson next asked how the pastors wished to carry on the meeting.

"We could break up into three or four small groups," someone suggested.

"That would squelch anyone from making a speech," Grace Dugan from Hemet advised. "This isn't a topic for loud speeches. Quiet, confidential sharing would be the most appropriate, wouldn't it?"

Cliff Benson, noted for old-fashioned oratory, sprang to his feet. "We all should hear what everyone says. I vote that we all stay together."

Dean Johnson lowered his head in thought, then turned toward the wall on his right. He stared a few moments at the large painting depicting the flight of Mary, Joseph and the baby Jesus into Egypt. Slowly shifting his eyes back to the pastors seated in a semi-circle of three rows, he offered his compromise. "How about small groups until lunch, then we all meet together till 2:00."

Seeing their faces indicated consent, Johnson asked everyone to count off by fours so that there could be four groups with five or six participants each. Joe's group proved to be an eye opener for him. No consensus could be achieved. Their experiences were too varied.

"When a young woman admitted she was gay, I suggested she see her doctor for help."

"Two gay men came to me and wanted me to marry them. When I said the law didn't permit it, they stormed out of my office."

"A devout young man confessed to me that he was gay, but he could be anything but gay in our church. I gave him a letter of transfer to a nearby Methodist church."

"I won't bless homosexual unions. The law gives them equal status, but that's no reason for the church to condone their life style."

When Joe's turn came, all he could say was that "There had been a very effeminate young college student in the Hiroshima church. Suddenly he stopped coming. My guess was that some member of the church teased him."

By noon, Dean Johnson sensed that none of the four groups had been successful in a positive way. They had only shared their differences. Everyone breathed a sigh of relief when the ladies in the kitchen rang a bell to call the pastors for lunch. Since the smell of pizza had wafted throughout the room, everyone was ready for the break. In eating they could be united, tasting the same flavor and joining in the same physical satisfaction. Over the meal no one steered the conversation back to sex.

At one o'clock the pastors assembled for their plenary session. The urgency of the discussion came home to all when one pastor told of a young gay man who'd come to him for counsel, but the pastor was unable to help him. A week later the man took his own life.

That led Grace Alone's Pastor Blomberg to tell of a woman in the church who divorced her husband when she discovered he had a gay partner.

"She's still suffering from the trauma of that," she confessed to me. "There are people in the pews who are really hurting. The problems often are deepseated and hidden from even their closest friends."

Veteran Pastor Elisen of Chino asked, "How should we prepare for the Synod meeting? Can we speak with one voice?"

Lots of talk ensued.

"Why don't we prepare a statement."

"Who can write it so it won't be misunderstood?"

"Do we have any lawyers who could help us?"

"Keep lawyers out it for now. They'll turn our words into legal jargon that no one will understand."

Finally Dean Johnson threw up his hands. "It's hopeless. Let's all go home and really examine the study documents. They have good biblical insights. God help us," Johnson concluded. "This is tough. Maybe our presiding national bishop can guide us. He's coming to the Synod convention."

An unknown voice in the back mumbled, "Can anything good come out of Milwaukee? Headquarters is always out of touch with California."

3
Telescopic Vision

On the drive home, Pastor Blomberg asked Joe, "How do you think we should discuss sexuality at Grace Alone?"

"What do you think, Aaron? You don't want to get caught in the middle. There are people with strong opinions on both sides."

"I've thought about it for a long while. Wouldn't the Mutual Ministry Committee be the place to begin?" Pastor Blomberg replied. "From there take it to the church council."

Hesitating to respond, Joe finally said, "I don't think as pastor you should chair the meetings. You'd have a hard time staying neutral."

The car turned into the Weavers' cul-de-sac and stopped in front of Joe's house. He didn't open the door. "Tough position for you to be in. You have to shepherd all the members — narrow and broadminded alike. Some take the biblical injunctions just as they are. Others believe our times are different from when *Leviticus* and *Romans* were written."

"We don't make women keep silent in church as in the first century," Pastor Blomberg said. "We don't think women have to keep their heads covered and mouths shut because that was the custom among the Jews 2000 years ago. The Christians then didn't want to ruffle feathers unnecessarily."

Joe nodded agreement. "Do not our Lutheran confessions teach that certain ideas and customs are *adiaphora*, meaning not essential to the faith. Another sticky point is smoking. When I went to seminary smoking was considered *adiaphora* — you could smoke or not smoke. It made no difference, like choosing the color of your necktie."

"Good point."

"I had a devout Baptist friend who had three pretty daughters. We fellows in high school gravitated to their house. I remember the mother, who spoke with a delightful Welsh accent, telling us, 'If God wanted people to smoke, he would have created them with a smokestack on top their heads.' Then twenty or thirty years later came the research that linked tobacco to lung cancer and other fatal diseases."

Pastor thought for a moment, then said, "Some research supports the value of having both fathers and mothers raise children."

"Yes, but the gay advocates say two men or two women can do just as good a job. It's hard to say anything for certain — too many variables, don't you think?"

"Joe, are you going to the Synod meeting?"

"Yes. It's close this year, so I can commute from home. I wouldn't want to miss this one. I may even contribute to the debate. Having lived overseas helps me see the big picture, at least I think it does."

"We certainly need light, no matter where it comes from. Well, Joe, I'd better let you go."

"Are you going to golf with us on Friday? You might want to sound out those laymen. They're practical, down-to-earth guys. Just don't ask them sex questions on their backswings. Wait for coffee time."

"Keep in touch. I'll let you go now." He waved as he backed the car out and turned to drive off.

Joe stood watching the young minister drive away. *Glad I'm not serving a church these days. I don't think I could handle it.*

As he opened the front door, the sound of Anita's harp drifted down the hall. "I'm home," he shouted, then walked toward the music. When his wife saw him enter her room, she stopped playing.

9

"Bill Scully didn't call while I was gone, did he?"

"No he didn't. How'd the meeting go?"

"Oh, so-so."

"What did the pastors say? Any consensus?"

"Their opinions are *samazama* (all over the place). I can't see how the Synod can speak with one voice."

"Do they have to say anything?"

"Everyone wants to give input to the national church convention in August, but ...."

Anita set the harp aside and moved closer to Joe. "Will you waste your time by attending Synod?"

"I wish I knew. One thing the meeting taught me was that I need to prepare better if I am to contribute anything."

"Did you feel welcome?"

Surprised by the question, he answered, "I think so, if for no other reason than my age. They seemed to listen when I spoke, but I'm not sure they understood me."

"That's nothing new. I can't understand you either — sometimes," she smiled. "After all, we're not from California; we're middle America at heart."

"On top of that, since we've worked in Japan for forty years," Joe said. "I can't blame them if we don't connect right away."

Anita looked at him. "That could be an advantage, you know."

"How so?"

"We see things from a distance. Do you recall the university professor who spoke about viewing objects in outer space?"

"Vaguely. What's the point?" .

"Remember how he said astronomers must use a telescope that gives the big picture. Once they've located what they're looking for, they switch to a more powerful telescope. Then they can make out the minute details."

Joe thought for a moment. "You're saying that I can function as a lens to show the large scene, then the others will have an easier time with the details."

"Yes, I think so. Give it some thought."

4
The Blow Up

Feeling drained of all energy, Joe retreated to the living room. The clock on the television read 3:00; so he decided to relax by watching "Home Improvement." Tim the Tool Man Taylor's souped up device for shooting insulation between the walls exploded, blowing cotton-like debris all over the room. It made Joe think that he himself might be over his head by trying to force a solution on sexuality issues. Trying too hard could cause more harm than good.

The telephone rang. He let it go, hoping that Anita would answer. After two rings, it stopped.

"Joe, telephone!"

Rather than take the call in his study, he went to the kitchen and picked up the portable phone. "Hello, who is this?" he asked.

"Bill Scully from the seminary."

"Hold on a second while I go to my chair." He sat down and picked up a pad of yellow paper. "Okay now. What's up?"

"Sally and I had a blowout yesterday."

Joe tried to react calmly. He recalled what he was taught in telephone counseling: "Act as a mirror for the caller. Reflect the client's image back to him." So, Joe spoke as smoothly as possible. "You had a blowout?"

"Yeah, it was pretty bad."

"Pretty bad, eh?"

"I took Sally for a walk to the colleges after lunch."

"Cold for a walk, wasn't it?"

"I knew where there was an alcove out of the wind, with a bench. We could sit and talk in private."

"That's good."

"When I began to express my doubts about our relationship, it backfired. She blamed herself for not showing enough affection. The more I tried to explain my misgivings, the more Sally came on to me. She'd never acted that way before. I think she was trying to prove how warm she could be."

"So, what happened?"

"She grabbed my shoulder and pushed her face into my lap. I should have shoved her off, but I didn't."

"You told me on Sunday that she was like a sister to you."

"She was no sister yesterday. Good God, she was wild. What should I have done?"

"I'm no expert, but it sounds as if she's not willing to give up on you — at least without a fight."

"How'd you feel about it?"

"Feel about it? She wouldn't let go. She made me come in my pants. That's never happened before."

"It sounds like you've got more than a sister. Did you still feel like her brother?"

Bill didn't respond.

"Are you okay, Bill?"

"I'm confused — thoroughly. I said she was like a sister to me, but last night — no matter how I tried to keep cool, I couldn't. She had become more than sister. God, I'm confused."

"I understand. When you're confused, your intuition might point you in the right direction."

"That's why I called you," Bill said, in an acusing tone.

"I appreciate that, but don't you have any hunches?"

"Like what?"

"Oh, for instance, talking to your mom and dad. Would you feel free to try that?"

Bill didn't respond. Joe suspected he had hit a sore spot. He waited before going further, surmising that Bill was on the verge of tears.

"Leave my mother and father out of this. They're separated. I haven't heard from my mother for over a year."

"And your father?"

"Dad checks up on me and once in a while sends money for school."

"Bill, I'm not a psychotherapist. I wouldn't want to get in too deep with you." Joe paused to weigh his next words carefully. "I could be very wrong. I think I can say that your feelings toward your mother might be predisposing you to feel discomfort toward women." *Did I say too much? What a stereotypical thought!*

"Doesn't the Bible say anything about this?" Bill asked. "There must be some help there."

Joe searched his memory. He hated simplistic answers. "I'm not sure how relevant Jesus' words about eunuchs are, but maybe they could shed some light. Hold on a second. I'll see if I can find the passage." He reached for his Bible. "It's somewhere in *Matthew*. I read it only last week. Here it is, Matthew 19:10-12."

His disciples said to him, "If such is the case of a man with his wife, it is better not to marry." But he said to them, "Not everyone can accept this teaching, but only to those to whom it is given. For there are eunuchs who have been so from birth, and there are eunuchs who have been made eunuchs by others, and there are eunuchs who have made themselves eunuchs for the sake of the kingdom of heaven. Let anyone accept this who can."

"So, he is saying that some have an inherent aversion to marriage. Others are that way because of environment, and others freely commit themselves to celibacy for the sake of the kingdom of God. That doesn't give you an answer, but it at least legitimizes three ways of dealing with it."

"I'm still mixed up," Bill said. "I know for now that I am not inclined toward celibacy, but was I born that way, or did circumstances shape me into what I am?"

13

"I'm thinking we need to find someone more knowledgeable than I am to help you sort this out."

"But who?"

"There's a trained counselor who rents a room at church. Would you mind if I ask her to recommend some expert to meet with you. I'd hate to give you bad advice."

Bill didn't respond immediately, but finally replied, "I suppose it wouldn't hurt. I've got to find out who I am."

"Okay then, I'll see what I can do. But we'll keep praying, and let's not forget Sally. Maybe I should meet her sometime. How about next Sunday after church?"

Bill paused, then said, "She can only refuse. I'll ask her. I think her Methodist church worships at 9:00; so she could come over to Grace Alone by 11:30."

"See you Sunday then. I'll try to have a name for you. Things are going to work out, work out just fine. Jesus won't let you down. Bye for now."

5
Lay Input

Tuesday morning Joe arose early. At 6:20, he left for the Claremont Golf Course. Because the ladies had competition on Tuesdays, most of the regular men didn't play. Only two other fellows from church showed up; so they played as a threesome and finished nine holes by 8:15. Then they headed to church for coffee.

A young woman was waiting on the patio for the professional counselor to arrive. Joe invited her to have some coffee, but she declined. He took a seat next to her on one of the unshaded benches. "Would you mind," he asked "if I speak with Mrs. Randolf, your counselor? I need to ask her a quick question."

"No problem."

Mrs. Randolph's gray Ford Taurus drove into the lot. Joe met her as she got out of the car. "Mrs. Randolph, I'm Joe Weaver from the church. I have a young seminary student who is torn up over his sexual orientation. I was wondering if you could recommend a psychotherapist, male if possible, who could see him."

"That should be possible. Come into the room. I'll give you a name: Dr. Jerry Fergeson."

"I appreciate this. I suspect the young man's strained relationship with his mother might have pushed him away from women. But I'm no expert. He took Dr. Fergeson's card from her. Thanks a lot. Sorry to have kept you and your client waiting."

He hurried into the kitchen, poured himself a cup of coffee and joined his two golf buddies in the little cubbyhole of a room beside the kitchen.

The two were discussing the church's broken sprinkler system. When their conversation slowed to a halt, Joe asked them, "Do you think anyone would object if Pastor Aaron married a couple of homosexuals?"

After an initial surprised look, Jay Glenwood said, "It isn't legal in California yet."

"Oh, I don't know," Stan Merkel objected. "If he did a simple blessing ceremony, what's wrong with that? It wouldn't break the law."

"Well then, could pastor announce it in the church bulletin and invite people to attend?"

"If he thinks it's the pastoral thing to do, why shouldn't he?" Stan asked.

"We call ourselves Grace Alone Church," Joe began, "but does that mean we condone everything? For instance, this is farfetched I know, but suppose you, Jay, get a crush on the choir director, could you ask the pastor to marry you, so that you can have two nice ladies to care for you in your old age?"

"That's going too far. Don't bring polygamy into the problem," Stan said.

"You have good ideas, Joe," Jay said, unconvincingly. "I don't think I'd do it."

Joe chuckled and then asked, "What about that pretty nurse who is coming to church now?"

Silence.

"Sorry I asked," Joe said. "I won't tell your wife. I think one wife is plenty for you."

Jay stood up and went to bring the coffee pot for refills. As he began pouring, Joe tried another question. "For the sake of discussion, suppose Pastor Aaron picks up and leaves. The bishop recommends a single graduate from Berkeley to replace him. The new man comes with high endorsement from his ethics professor and the president of the seminary. But at the bottom of the letter, the bishop has added a footnote saying he is a homosexual and might want to live with his partner. The ordination ceremony would be expected to take place at Grace Alone. What do you think we should do?"

"You're ruining my coffee," Stan said. "We'd need to consider a lot of things."

"For instance?" Joe asked.

"Take the secretary. She's not a member here, but comes from a conservative Baptist church. There's the Sunday School and Boy Scouts. How would our youth minister and the troop leader react? Is there any way we can sound them out?"

Stan set his coffee down and began tapping the table with his fingers. "We'd also need to find out what his work experience has been. Did he do well?"

"I'm sorry," said Joe. "I didn't mean to spoil our coffee time, but I am troubled. Yesterday at the Mt. Baldy ministers' meeting, opinions were all over the place. This May the sexuality issues will be on the Synod's agenda. I'm going, and I want to be constructive. What's best for congregations, for our communities, and for our outreach? Give it some thought. Next Friday after golf let's talk about it again. Maybe the other guys who come can help us."

"Good idea," Jay said. "Maybe I'll ask pastor what the nurse's name is." He broke up laughing before he finished the sentence.

"See you Friday. I'm going to borrow pastor's study to make a phone call. See you later."

Joe went to Pastor Blomberg's desk. He picked up the phone and started to punch in Dr. Fergeson's numbers, but abruptly stopped. He put the phone down, bent over and rested his forehead on the desk. He began praying silently that this Dr. Fergeson would agree to meeting Bill Scully.

Lifting his head, Joe again began to call the doctor. On the fifth ring, a sonorous male voice answered, "Hello, this is Dr. Fergeson, what may I do for you?"

Relieved by the deep, pleasant tone of the doctor's voice, Joe went straight to the point, even sharing information about the bench episode. "Do you think you could see Mr. Scully to determine if it would be worth his while to take professional counseling?"

Joe arranged to go with Bill to meet him at the Foothill Institute where Fergeson goes on Monday afternoons.

"That's great. We'll see you then about 5:00 on Monday. I really appreciate your willingness to see Bill. He's a young man with a great future."

Joe hung up, then telephoned Bill to confirm the appointment. "Hallelujah!" he shouted. He felt they were on the right path.

6
GLEE

The rattling of mail being stuffed into the mailbox woke Joe from his nap. *What time is it? Boy, she's early today.*

He went to open the door to greet the mail carrier. "Thanks! Hope you didn't bring any more bills."

"Looked like a pile of them. Sorry, I'm not allowed to throw them away."

The mailbox was so full, Joe had to use both hands to wiggle everything out. *Five catalogues. No wonder we're losing the rain forests!*

He went to the dining room table and separated the daily supply of environmental fund appeals, political flyers and advertisements from the real letters. On the bottom was a letter to him from an organization called "GLEE." He tore it open, curious to find out what GLEE stood for. It wasn't a printed ad, but one of those computer-generated personal letters. At the top it said in large letters "GLEE," with smaller print below. "Gays and Lesbians for Evangelical Equality."

> "Dear Pastor Weaver," the letter began.
>
> "Or should I call you 'Joe?' It was good to meet you at the Mt. Baldy Conference meeting and learn how interested you are in seeing justice achieved for us gays and lesbians."

From there the letter obviously was a form letter added to the personalized first paragraph.

"Knowing of your sympathetic attitudes toward Lutherans who advocate for equality for persons of all sexual orientations, we invite you to sign the enclosed petition to be submitted to the 2004 Synod Assembly in May. Please sign the form and solicit signatures from friends at your church. Mail the completed form back to us at the Newport Beach address on the stamped envelope provided.

"Thank you for taking this step for justice.

"Sincerely in Christ,
The GLEE Committee"

The names of about ten men and women were then listed, none of whom Joe knew personally.

He turned the page over to examine the resolution itself, which was very concise, leaving lines for signatures on the bottom of the page.

To: The Assembly of the Southern California Synod Concordia Lutheran Church-USA.

We the undersigned petition the Synod Assembly to consider favorably the following resolutions:

Whereas Christ's Gospel is for all men and women, it behooves our beloved church to uniquivocally express that welcoming spirit in word and deed.

Therefore, we implore our Synod to advocate to the 2004 Biennial Assembly of the national church that it grant the clergy of our church permission to perform weddings for persons of the same sex just as they now do for couples of the opposite sex.

Also, we petition the Synod to recommend that the national church rescind its ban on the ordaining of non-celibate gays and lesbians.

Joe scratched his head, knowing he had not advocated this at the conference meeting. *Maybe my empathetic tone gave that impression.*

He picked up a pen and scribbled a note on the lines reserved for supporters of the petition. "Thanks for including me on your mailing list. It is very commendable that you are stating your positions and making what amounts to motions that can be acted on promptly. Since I am still studying the issues, you will understand why I am unable to sign the petition. My hunch is that there may be aspects to the issues which have not been addressed yet.

"Thank you, anyway"

Joe hesitated before writing his name. Then to hedge his stance, he did not sign his full name, but only wrote Joe.

"Good God, help us. The issues are so complex, yet so simple to some people.

"Hey, Ani, come here. I want to show you something."

"Wait a minute. It's time to go to lunch." She came in the room, and Joe showed her the letter and how he had responded.

She speed-read it and handed it back to him. "If that's how you feel, that's how you feel. You're civil enough."

"I hope so. This issue is sapping all my energy. There are too many facets to the problem. I believe I can help, but how?"

Anita slipped into her shoes. As she went out the door, she looked back at Joe. "You've got to stop thinking about sex all the time."

"I'm sorry," he sighed, loudly. Then he put his shoes on and trotted to catch up with her.

7
Islamic Input

Still remembering Anita's chiding over sex, Joe entered the dining hall, checked to see what their table number was. His wife had stopped to chat with someone and had not come to the table yet. Opposite them sat two new residents, Richard Mellinger and his wife Margaret.

After Anita took her seat and two single ladies, Jean Harell and Thelma Burns, filled in the remaining two places, Joe started the process of getting everyone introduced.

"I was absent the day you two were welcomed in the dining room. Tell us about yourselves. Anita and I are part of what some call 'the Japanese mafia.'"

"Mafia?" Margaret asked with a puzzled look.

"It's because here we have about forty former Japan missionaries. Most of us went to Japan after World War II and retired about the same time. Where did you work?"

"Our last tour of duty was in the Cameroons," Richard replied. "Before that, Nigeria."

"How exciting!" Jean said.

"Exciting is an understatement," Mrs. Mellinger said. "Try raising kids in such unsettling surroundings."

Thelma, who had been a teacher in Turkey, nodded and asked, "Were any of your children girls?"

"All girls," Richard replied.

"They stood out like sore thumbs," Margaret added. "They were blond like me. But stubborn like Richard. They wouldn't cover their heads like the Muslims."

"Girls complained of harassment," Thelma said. "Can you imagine it, more than once I had my bottom pinched." She laughed loudly.

"Coffee, anyone?" Anita asked.

The dinner bell sounded, then a woman's voice offered a prayer.

Thelma began filling the plates and passed them around. "You can eat after two are served," Joe explained. "It's rule 36, or is it 37? Lots of unwritten rules. You'll get used to them. It took me only five years to adjust."

Mrs. Mellinger turned to Jean, "and where have you served?"

"Only in this country. My husband and I pastored congregations in Wyoming, Colorado, and near San Jose, California. John died six months ago."

"That must have been hard," Margaret said.

"We average about eighteen deaths a year here. Very sobering," said Joe. For a while that dampened conversation.

"I have a question. You've worked with Muslims, haven't you? Is there a big problem with AIDS?"

"You would ask that," Richard replied.

"I saw a TV segment about Senegal, a Muslim country. They claim there are few HIV infections because of strict rules about sex. Did you find that so?"

Margaret answered. "Maybe not as true as in Senegal, but, Richard, wouldn't you say Muslims have less AIDS?"

"I think so."

"Heavy stuff," Joe continued, "but how do Muslims regard homosexuality? Sorry, ladies, I hope you don't mind my curiosity."

"Lunches here are going to be stimulating," Richard said.

"They told us,"Anita said, "that talk about theology and politics during meals was taboo."

Richard hesitated. "My answer may touch on theology. Okay?" The others nodded.

"I've studied it some. The *Koran*, deals with this. In fact my copy of it has a fairly extensive index of topics."

"Really," Anita said.

"For instance?" Joe asked.

"They make much of the story about Abraham's nephew, Lot, who went to Sodom. Lot told the Sodomites, 'You lust after men instead of women. Truly, you are a degenerate people.'"

Turning to Anita, Joe said, "That's where the word *sodomy* comes from, isn't it?"

"Everyone knows that," his wife retorted.

"In another place," Richard continued, "'If two men among you commit a lewd act, punish them both.'"

"It sounds like you've memorized a lot of Koran verses," said Thelma. "I never read it with that much care."

"There's much more detail in other passages, accusing the people in Sodom of lewd acts and abominations. No other nations committed the lewd acts the Sodomites did. So, they deserved God's destruction."

"I guess I should study it. Do you think our library has a copy in English? Or, maybe I should check with the leader of the mosque over in Pomona. I'll want to talk with you more about this. Do you mind if I call you Dick?"

"Dick? No one's dared call me that since I went to Nigeria."

Joe shook his head. "Really? I can see there's a lot I don't understand about Islamic culture."

On the way home, Joe stopped at the library. Checking the card catalogue, he found the Koran listed and was pleased to find it in the stacks. It was published under Penguin Classics. It had a glossy cover with Arabic script on it.

Flipping to the back of the book to see who had checked it out before, he was surprised to find no names. *Am I the only resident curious enough to read the Muslims' holy book.* Looking at the back pages, he was delighted to find a twenty-page topical index with five entries devoted to homosexuality. He signed out for the book and headed home, glad that he'd worn a sweater, because the sky had clouded over, and a chilly breeze was blowing in from the west. As soon as he entered the house, he turned on the heat.

Instead of stretching out for a nap, he switched on the reading lamp and began looking up pertinent passages. His sudden zeal in searching the Muslim scriptures reminded him of his own spiritual awakening as a youth when he couldn't get enough of the Bible. He recalled how he'd argued with his Mormon pal. One time he even drew in a Catholic priest to back him up about marriages in heaven.

Joe was surprised to see how different the Koran was from the Bible. To him it tended to be didactic and preachy in contrast to the Bible's stories and historical accounts. He realized that he'd need much more background before he could really appreciate it.

Now all he wanted were the exhortations about sexuality. He jotted down a few notes and page numbers for future reference. It all seemed like heavy reading, so he set the book aside. He pulled himself out of his chair and stepped out on the porch to clear his head. Seeing the watering can, he carried it to the kitchen to fill, then returned to water the plants lined up on the railing.

The one passage he liked was about wives being created for husbands. He could understand how they were a gift to men, but he knew that idea wouldn't fly very high with American feminists. *Strange how the same fact can be interpreted differently, depending on one's position or environment. Anita has certainly been a blessing to me, and so have the children. In my heart I don't mind her scolding me once in a while about being untidy. I'll never forget the musty smell and dusty mess in some widowers' homes. How lonely must they be on their down days!*

Thinking about what he'd read, Joe speculated whether or not Muslim scholars questioned these stern admonitions as only applicable for ancient settings. Are they divided on such questions as much as Christians?

Just then, he noticed that a gust of wind blew open the Stars and Stripes in front of the house, fifty white stars held together on a cloth of blue. He pondered whether the fifty states have enough in common to hold them together, or are we becoming two nations divided by religious and cultural differences?

Joe went on to soliloquize about his own beloved Concordia Lutheran Church. Can we maintain the necessary concord in love, or will the fissures become so deep that love no longer can bridge the chasm? What role, if any, can I play — a mere shooting star or a calm adhesive holding the extremes together? I'm only one person, retired at that, but help me, Lord, to reach out my arms wide enough to embrace all. Or, am I only day dreaming wishful thoughts? Don't let me be so narrow, Lord, that I become invisible. Give me a place, no matter how small, where I can count for something.

Closing his eyes, Joe realized that the stringent commands in the Muslims' holy book had surprised him. How in the world did they decide what was lewd? He didn't want to deal with that now, so he put his mind in neutral. Sleep soon overtook him. He didn't stir until Anita began using the telephone. His watch said 3:30. While he slept, the mail had arrived. He wondered whether there might be some new message for him.

8
Surprise Visitor

The only genuine message that came was a blue post-card from the Synod office, the way for announcing a pastor's memorial service.

"Who has died now?" Joe asked himself as he lifted up the card. Death notices usually did not mean anything to him personally because he didn't know most of the California pastors. But it wasn't a funeral announcement. It was the notification that the Reverend Shinichi Katsunaga had arrived to serve the Japanese congregation in Yorba Linda. *Katsunaga* sounded familiar. It was very uncommon, so Joe questioned if it might be a relative of his former co-worker in East Hiroshima.

Joe had often told the story of that Katsunaga's experience in the Pacific War. During the last hopeless days for the Japanese, Katsunaga had been chosen to give his life in a suicidal attack against the U.S. navy, not as a *kamikaze* fighter pilot but on a one-man torpedo. He failed to reach his target and was left abandoned at sea. All he had left for food was a can of beans, but no can opener. He drifted for several days, growing weaker and weaker. In frantic desperation he gnawed the tin open and was able to survive till he was rescued.

He became Joe's helper in the mid-1950s. In their visitations to a tuberculosis sanitarium, Katsunaga contracted the disease. Joe also was infected but never fell ill.

As Joe contemplated what possible significance this new Japanese pastor might have for him, he read the rest of the postcard. At the bottom it listed Katsunaga's telephone number. Joe was tempted to call him at once, but his own phone rang. He picked it up and answered.

"Is Rev. Weaver home?" the male voice on the line asked in a noticeable Japanese accent.

"This is Rev. Weaver."

"You don't know me, but my father told me about you."

"You're not the Hiroshima Katsunaga's grandson, are you?"

"Yes. I've come to be pastor at the St. Paul Church in Yorba Linda. I would like to talk with you about the American church."

"We'll have to get together," Joe said. "I'm anxious to hear all about you and the family. Are you married?"

"Yes, of course. The Japanese Church won't send anyone not married. Is it alright to visit you with my wife and baby?"

"How's Thursday afternoon about 3:00?"

"*Subarashii!* (Great)

After Joe gave him directions to the house, they said, "Goodbye." Joe leaned back in his chair and stared at the ceiling. He reached for his prayer book and read the noon prayer for Tuesdays, but the words fell flat. He needed something that fit his situation now, so he gave up on words and trusted silence to be his prayer.

On the fourth of February, Joe regretted that he had not gone golfing. He fidgeted from one household task to another. Even after a brisk walk before noon and a shower, he couldn't shake his uneasines. He wondered if the coming of the Katsunaga family wasn't putting him on edge.

During lunch, a table companion remarked about the latest issue of *Time,* which was a special about sex. Joe felt tempted to ask to borrow it, but hesitated. Instead, he drove over to Borders to buy his own copy.

Since he was not in the habit of browsing through the rows of magazine sections, he failed to find it. He went to the information counter for help, but bumped into an acquaintance standing there. Joe waited until his friend left before he asked the clerk to direct him to where he could find the magazine. She led him straight to the one display case he hadn't seen.

"There it is," she said, and left him. Joe picked up the magazine and quickly pressed it against his chest, front cover facing in. He continued to hug it while he waited at the check-out counter. The woman cashier took the magazine from him and swiped it across the scanner. Her eyes brightened, giving Joe an impish look. He knew she'd read the front cover: HOW YOUR LOVE LIFE KEEPS YOU HEALTHY. He tried his best to look like one of those male models in the Viagra ads.

"Do you want a bag?"

"Yes, I'd better have one, don't you think?" If he had a tail, now would have been the time to tuck it between his legs.

When he arrived home, he shoved the bag under his chair.

That evening, he watched the seven o'clock news over CNN. At the end, Aaron Brown read some headlines from the Thursday morning papers. He held up the *Los Angeles Chronicle* for viewers to see.

Massachusetts Grants Gays Right to Marry

The landmark court ruling makes it the first state to uphold full rights for same-sex couples, not civil unions and similar separate arrangements

"Oh, my God, the pressure keeps coming," Joe muttered. "This will make it tricky for the churches."

He poured himself a second glass of Burgundy, hoping that would make him sleep more soundly. But his strategy backfired. He had to go to the toilet three times during the night. After the last trip down the hall at 4:00 a.m., he couldn't get back to sleep. He played back from memory every word spoken at the Mt. Baldy pastors' meeting. In his heart he wanted to believe that the church eventually would reach a consensus. He believed the words from the Apostles Creed: "I believe in the Holy Spirit, the holy Christian church, the communion of saints." Not concerned about waking his wife, he recited the words aloud again, and added, "I believe; I believe."

But his fidgeting did not abate, so he got out of bed and went to the recliner, his holy place. There all indecisions could be resolved, but today they weren't.

As usual he left home at 6:30 to play golf with his Eternally Young partners. For the first three holes the February wind chilled them to the bone. When the sun came up, Joe shed his windbreaker and let the sun warm his arms. On every hole his putter failed so that by the 15th, he hadn't won a single skin.

"We know you, Joe." Ken Ostrood kidded. "You always wait for the last holes when the skins are worth more."

"You guys are too tough for me today," Joe replied. But inside he vowed to win the last three holes, worth an imaginary $450,000.

He teed up his ball first to make a statement that would put pressure on the others. His drive sped off, but too low, clipping a branch on the far side of the barranca.

"You went down," Ostrood said.

"No, I think I cleared. I won't play a provisional."

After crossing over the gully, Don helped look for the ball, but soon threw up his hands. "No luck," he said.

"Oh, here it is," Joe shouted, "right on the out-of-bounds line. I think I can play it, if I don't slide down and break my neck." He dug his spikes into the slope, reminding him of other slippery slopes. Blotting distractions from his mind, Joe hit a lofty flyer onto the green and two-putted to tie for low ball.

Buoyed by that, he knew his luck had turned. *If I can only stay focused, I can win the skins game.* But at that instant, sharp pain shot through the toes of his left foot, making him limp.

"What's wrong, Joe?" Ostrood asked.

"Nothing. I'll be okay."

"Do you want to go up to the clubhouse and wait for us?"

"Quit, and let you fellows win the big skins? Never!"

Puffing up the hill through the long wet rough, he reached the tee out of breath. He leaned on his driver to rest his legs and gazed north toward the17th green. He took several deep breaths. "I must keep going, one stroke at a time."

He managed to tie the 17th hole, but cleaned up three skins on the18th, worth $450,000. Then, true to form, Joe theologized about his victory. He believed golf to be the ideal metaphor for the pursuit of perfection.

For the rest of the morning, the high he had experienced on the golf course stayed with him. Katsunaga, Haruko, his wife, and Ken-chan, their infant son, arrived right on time in the afternoon.

Joe went out to the curb to welcome them. "Three o'clock sharp, you're as prompt as a Japanese train."

"This is Haruko; that's Ken-chan asleep in the car seat," Shinichi said.

Anita came out to invite them into the house. "Good thing you came today. The cleaning lady was here this morning. Joe had to clean up the mess around his chair before she arrived."

Pointing to the couch, Joe said, "Take a seat. Do you drink coffee? Or, would you prefer tea?"

"Coffee is fine," Shinichi replied.

Anita brought in a tray with coffee and almond bars. "Do you use sugar and cream?"

"No thanks. Black is fine."

"Most Japanese like some sugar and cream," Anita said.

"We've lost track of your grandparents. Are they still living?" Joe asked.

"No, they both died over twenty years ago and are interred in the family plot in Kumamoto."

"Did your folks live down there, too?"

"We both grew up there, not too far from Kumamoto Castle."

"What about school?" Anita asked.

"Haruko went to Kyushu JoGakuin girls school, and I went to the boys school, then seminary in Tokyo. Haruko studied in the social welfare division. That's where we met."

"It's quite a big step for you to come to the States. How do you feel about the Church's sending you here?"

Shinichi sucked in his breath, slow to answer. "It scares me."

"Scares you?" Anita asked.

"Everything here feels different, not just outwardly. Maybe *fuan* (unrest) is how to describe it."

"Hmm, would *ambivalence* be a good word for it?" Joe asked. "Some good and some bad."

"Our church members in Yorba Linda are a mixture. Half were born here. They're very American. Quite frank, even rude to our ears at first."

Haruko added, "We've been told that men from Japan work all week and play golf on Sunday. Few come to church, except when their kids perform at Christmas."

"Give yourself time," Anita said. "We even took a while before we felt at home in America again."

"Five years for me," Joe said. "I've finally stopped bowing on the phone. When you called the other day, you sounded anxious to talk about the American church and its problems."

"Excuse me, Haruko, would you like to see the rest of the house? You can leave the baby here. I want to show you my harp."

Haruko leaned the car seat against the sofa and followed Anita to the back.

Turning to Shinichi, Joe asked, "Is there anything special on your mind?"

Shinichi appeared shy to ask, but then said, "Sometime I'd like for someone to explain your presidential election. Candidates look so angry. My members seem divided, but no one talks about it in church." He reached into his coat pocket and pulled out a notebook.

"Best way to learn about that is through the newspapers and TV, especially cable. There are lots of talk shows and panel discussions which present all sides of the issues."

"At our board meeting at St. Paul's last week, two members shocked me. They asked me what I'd do if two gays asked me to marry them."

"Already? My word, can't people wait till you're settled."

"The seminary in Tokyo didn't teach us about that. I can't remember any talk about it, except once. And that was at Tokyo

Union Seminary when a visiting American professor lectured, but no one raised any questions."

"That's troubling many of us here. Our national church is making a four-year study of sexuality issues. I'm not sure how it will come out. People are very divided. They should decide next August after the final report is presented."

"How should I handle it?"

"You can say you've been told that it's against the law in California to perform same-sex weddings. That won't settle the matter, but it will give you time to wait for the national church to settle on a policy."

"Isn't that legalistic?"

"I know. That's our dilemma. Can love be tough, and unkind?" Joe said. "I'm struggling over this, too. Many in our churches are worried. Our local Mt. Baldy Conference can't agree on a position — at least, not yet."

"Do you think I could come back alone some day, so we could talk about it a little longer?"

"Good idea! Thursdays are open for me usually. How about lunch on Thursday, the 12th? I can show you the seminary in Upland and the Claremont Village. That's a great place to relax and talk over coffee. I'll try to get some reading materials ready for you. I want to hear what you think."

9
Valentine's Day

The displays of Valentine cards at the supermarket turned Joe off. The verses never expressed what he'd want to tell Anita. He told himself that he'd write a few lines of sweet prose or a Japanese *haiku* that would come from his heart. But by the time his wife left for a weekend harp workshop in San Diego, he had written nothing except a checklist for her, including her medicines, toothbrush and lastly, clean underwear.

Even if she didn't catch his humor, he kept trying. But it was no joke that his final farewell finished with, "Drive defensively. When you stop to eat, make sure no one follows you to the car."

After lunch, he settled in for a quiet afternoon of reading, ending with the sending of an E-mail to the family. He had nothing in particular to write about, so he listed the subject as "Home Alone." The quietness of the house made him sympathize with widowers who had lost their wives. He could face up to three days alone, but knew indefinite aloneness would be horrendous. He often uttered his vow to outlive his wife. It was not only an excuse to justify his playing golf four times a week.

He had heard of a college student who exclaimed, "Isn't it boring?" to his professor who had been married thirty-five years. That young man didn't know what marriage was all about. Joe knew he and Anita were in many respects opposites, but that enhanced their lives. The *yin-yang* principle held much truth for him. Then he tried to recall Elizabeth Barrett Browning's sonnet of love about Robert, her husband. *If only I were a poet, I'd write something like hers.*

He stood up and went to his book shelves and returned carrying a book of poetry. Thumbing through the pages, he came to a dog-eared one containing the favorite sonnet by Mrs. Browning, which read:

How do I love thee? Let me count the ways.

I love thee to the depth and breadth and height

My soul can reach, when feeling out of sight

For the ends of Being and ideal Grace.

The last two lines, Joe hoped, he could make his own words some day.

Smiles, tears, of all my life! — and, if God choose,

I shall but love thee better after death.

Joe bowed his head and sat in silence.

That evening he shoved aside his loneliness by watching the news. He felt bored by all the hullabaloo over President Bush's National Guard service and John Kerry's photo with Jane Fonda. So what? Maybe it would be best, he thought, for the country to elect someone who had the foresight to see that the Vietnam War was a mistake, or was it? His Malaysian friend was sincere when he thanked Joe on behalf of America for saving his country. He thought Southeast Asia could have fallen into a chaos that might have outdone Chairman Mao's Cultural Revolution in China.

When Joe went to bed, little did he realize what a surprise February 14th would bring. With nothing on his agenda for that Saturday, he slept in until 7:00. He put the tea kettle on to heat, then went out to fetch the morning paper. He brought it in and opened it on the dining room table. At the top of the front page he saw a colored photo of a long line of couples waiting for marriage licenses at the City Hall in San Francisco. To the left it stated that "San Francisco Wins Round 1 in Marriage Battle." Below, it said that a Superior Court judge had denied an injunction against allowing gay couples to wed.

Joe wondered how this cultural war would play out in the churches. In spite of the so-called separation of church and state, on questions of marriage the two had been linked in mutual understanding ever since the founding of the nation. But if the state now changes its rules, how should the church respond?

He read the rest of the first page which ended by pointing out that Mayor Gavin Newsom had acted contrary to state law. This provoked an attorney with the Alliance Defense Fund to label the action "municipal anarchy."

Turning to the rest of the story, he opened to page A28. There he was confronted by a huge photo of head-scarved members of the Islamic group Al-Sabeel holding high a huge sign proclaiming: "Homosexuality is a major sin!!!"

"Yappari! (as I thought) They're only saying what the Koran teaches." Joe could guess how this news might be playing out among his friends in Malaysia and Indonesia. There the Christians survive as minorities in a sea of Muslims. Prayers for his friends raced through his mind as he poured tea into his mug. He only hoped that someone would be there for them, making sense out of the news from America. They need to know that California approved by 61 percent in 2000 Proposition 22. That added to the California Family Code that "only marriage between a man and a woman is valid or recognized in California."

The foundations may be eroding. What a field day the lawyers will have! And the theologians. I would sure love to sit in with the Fuller Seminary professors when they begin their dialogue with Muslim leaders next month.

The telephone rang. It was Anita. "I arrived safely. Last night the program lasted past 10:00, so I didn't call you."

"Enjoy! I already miss you. It was chilly last night so I added an extra blanket. You forgot to tell me which necktie to wear on Sunday."

"Do the best you can. Sorry. I've got to run. The others are waiting."

10
San Francisco Fallout

On Sunday, Joe had ample time to ponder what had been transpiring in his life. He even felt exhilarated over John Daly's victory at Torrey Pines in the Buick Open. It had been almost ten years since Daly had won a U.S. tournament. In spite of family conflicts and struggles with addiction, Daly had overcome. He bested the young local favorite, Chris Riley, and Luke Donald. In spite of all his difficulties, Daly had hung in to win.

With Sunday being a great encouragement for Joe, he relaxed thoroughly in the evening until Anita arrived home safely. With thanks for a perfect day of rest, he slept very soundly. All this sense of well being continued during his morning nine holes at the Claremont course. None of his church buddies showed up, so Joe played solo, at peace with nature and himself.

At home when he sat down for breakfast, the ringing of the phone broke his euphoric spell.

"Is this Pastor Weaver's residence?" a female voice asked.

"This is Pastor Weaver."

"I'm Peggy, Dean Johnson's secretary. We've got an emergency in the Mt. Baldy Conference. Dean Johnson wants all clergy to meet at 10:00 Tuesday at Bethany Church in Ontario. That's all. Hope you can make it."

Before Joe could ask any questions, the secretary had hung up, leaving him with a mixture of shock and apprehension.

"This is unprecedented. It must be urgent, to call a meeting on such short notice. The conference has no legal authority to make binding decisions on the church, so what gives?" he asked himself.

After breakfast, Joe napped for twenty minutes, then woke bright and ready to face the day. Since it was Presidents Day, he felt no guilt over taking his time to read the paper. He devoured the front-page account of the many hundreds of gay and lesbian couples weathering the rain to get marriage licenses in San Francisco.

He was consternated over the eagerness of people to take this action of civil disobedience against the law. But Joe did qualify his objections when he recalled how he himself had spoken out in defense of Martin Luther King's civil disobedience to right racial injustice.

"How will the lawyers ever sort this out?" he said to Anita.

"Sort what out?"

"These marriages okayed by San Francisco. Dean Johnson is even asking the Mt. Baldy clergy to meet tomorrow."

"About what?" she asked.

"I don't know. Maybe it would be worth a call to him. I don't want to go unprepared."

He went to the kitchen for the phone and Synod directory. He stood at the counter and punched in the dean's number.

"Hello, Henry, this is Joe Weaver. What's this meeting tomorrow all about. Why the hurry?"

"Haven't you seen the morning paper? Look in the *Chronicle,* California section, page B2. That's what the meeting is about."

"I was reading the paper, but hadn't got that far."

"All you need is right there under the photo. Hope that satisfies you. See you tomorrow."

"Yes, see you tomorrow." Joe slowly set the phone back on its cradle, fearful over what he'd see in the paper.

"It's all on page two of the California section," he said to Anita as he hurried back to the dining room to look at B2.

Two familiar faces greeted him from the page: Tillie Van Pelt and Roxanna Bovard. The caption under their names read: "Two long-time couples receive a wedding license." When interviewed, they said, "This is only legal approval. We are asking our minister to perform a church wedding for us."

"*Naruhodo* (I understand now). That puts their pastor in a fine fix. He must have asked the dean to get the area clergy to give him counsel."

"What do you think the pastors will say?" Anita asked.

"Oh, God, what a time to be a pastor — shepherd for the whole flock. Wolves are after the sheep. How hard to see who they are. For all we know, we might be the wolves. What a thought! Heaven help us. We sure need superhuman wisdom."

11
The Bishop Comes

Joe awoke with an eery sense that Jesus was walking ahead of him. He didn't know what it meant. Only as he followed one step at a time would the way become clear. Fretting served no purpose; it would only disorient him.

Since KUSC was doing its winter fund raising, he didn't turn on the radio, but opted for a recording of Bach's B minor Mass. The intricate interweaving of vocal solos with a violin and full orchestra fascinated him. When the chorus began singing the Sanctus, he pushed the recliner back and let the music fill his soul. He knew that if he could ride that music, the rest of the day would be easy.

On the way to Ontario, he listened to Schubert's Unfinished Symphony. That brought back memories of an "ancient" film he saw in his teens. It depicted the romantic story of that music and how the composer never was able to complete it. How sad, Joe thought, to leave a work unfinished.

When he drove into the Bethany parking lot, another car pulled up next to his.

"Glad you're here,"said the voice of Pastor Hansen.

"How are you doing, David?"

"What's this meeting about? The dean has never called an urgent one like this before."

"It's about those two women in the photo the *Chronicle* ran. That's all I know."

For such a late notice, Joe was surprised to see the parish hall filled. In typical Scandinavian custom, the ladies of the church had cooked a big pot of coffee and laid out a spread of donuts and cookies.

Joe had heard that neighbors called Bethany "The Restaurant with the Cross on Top."

It reminded him of his Japanese church that always had tea and coffee available before worship. The pastor claimed that was the only way he could keep the members awake during the sermon. After Joe filled his cup and grabbed a donut, he looked for an open seat. Just then, Bishop Alfred Friberg came through the door. Hansen poked Joe in the arm, "Oh boy, even the Synod bishop is here. He's never attended our conference meetings before."

"Now that our bishop has arrived," Dean Johnson announced, would you all take your coffee and sit down. We need to stay on schedule."

When everyone had found a place, Johnson invited Cliff Benson, the most senior active minister to open the meeting with prayer. He stood up. In a booming bass voice, he intoned petitions of great urgency.

Then Dean Johnson spoke. "I've called you here today to clarify our church's policy and give counsel to one of our pastors who has asked for your help. You may have seen the photo of the two women who received their marriage license last Saturday in San Francisco. What you may not know is that those two ladies are members of St. Luke's in Yucaipa, where Pastor Jose Gonzales serves. Normally Jose insists on a least five counseling sessions, the recommended practice for our churches. These two women already have their license and are asking Jose to perform the Rite of Holy Matrimony immediately. We realize that Governor Schwarzenegger or the courts may declare same-sex marriages illegal." Turning to Pastor Gonzales, he asked, "Is that correct?"

"Basically so," Gonzales replied, "but I'm confused."

"We need to back up," Dean Johnson said. "Could we ask Bishop Friberg to explain what regulations our church has in place now. Let's begin there."

After a few words of appreciation for being invited, the bishop read what the church's current policy and practice are:

"All people are welcome in Lutheran congregations, but this church has no policy on the blessing of same-sex unions."

"Haven't the bishops expressed their judgements about this?" someone asked.

"Yes, I think you're referring to what the bishops said a decade ago. Wait a second. I have a copy of that. He reached into his briefcase and pulled out a transparent folder containing the statement. "Let me read it."

"We bishops have not approved any official ceremony for blessing same-sex unions because we found no basis for it in the Bible or in tradition. Our statements, however, do not establish policy but do shape its understandings and practice."

Dean Johnson pointed to a hand in back. Joe didn't recognize the man, who then asked, "Wasn't that a cop out? What do you think, Bishop Friberg?"

"At that time I wasn't a bishop. My understanding is that the bishops did not want to usurp the authority of the national Assembly. That's why they struck a moderate tone.

"I should add that in the Guidelines for Discipline, it's stated that 'it is the policy of the Concordia Lutheran Church that all single rostered clergy, including those who understand themselves to be homosexual, are expected to abstain from sexual relationahips.'"

Cliff Benson, known for being a stickler, raised his voice, "And what is a sexual relationship?"

Someone laughed and said, "You ought to know by now."

"I'm serious," Benson shot back. "Do we make it narrow, the so-called Clintonian interpretation. Do we include hanky-pancky sexual games? What about addiction to pornography like that Harvard professor who got fired?"

"I can see we're going far afield. The immediate problem we face is what advice can we give Pastor Gonzales. If we follow the present guidelines, I don't think he can perform a church ceremony for two women."

"But times have changed," Pastor Grace Dugan shouted. "We know much more than we did ten years ago."

"That still doesn't trump Scripture and two thousand years of tradition," Joe said. "We need to help Jose and his two parishioners."

Dean Johnson looked at Jose. "What's your gut feeling about this?"

Jose got up, turned around to face his colleagues. "I'm deeply troubled. If I gave the women a Christian wedding, my Hispanic members would be upset, maybe even leave the church, even though they care a great deal about the ladies. Some younger Anglos wouldn't object. But then there's California law. It's a no-win situation."

"Can't you do a private ceremony, not using official liturgy?" Hansen proposed.

"I've suggested that to them, but they insist on a public ceremony and a big reception in the fellowship hall."

Bishop Friberg slowly took the floor. "You have an impossible predicament. I may sound like Gamaliel, the Pharisee who cautioned the Jewish authorities about jailing the apostles. Didn't he say, 'You could find yourselves fighting against God!' The court has given Mayor Gavin Newsom until March 29 to defend his action disregarding the ban on same-sex marriages. That gives you, Pastor Gonzales, breathing room. I suggest you stick to the church guidelines that call for a least five counseling sessions. Tell the women that your bishop insists on it. By the time you've had five weeks with the women, the air may be clear enough so that you can see your solution."

Joe turned his head around and said to Pastor Saulgren, "I can see why we need a bishop."

Dean Johnson faced Pastor Gonzales and asked him, "How does that sound?"

"Very simple. Why didn't I think of that?"

"You're too close to the problem," Johnson said. "Isn't there a proverb that says, 'The foot of the lighthouse is the darkest.'

"We've had a fruitful morning. Thank you bishop. Let's all stand and sing the Doxology." A lady's voice pierced through the music, "Before you leave, help us clean up the goodies."

12
Student Voices

The telephone rang as Joe opened the front door. "Ani, can you get that?" he yelled toward the back of the house.

"It's for you," she called back.

"Hello. This is Joe Weaver."

"Bill Scully here. I need your help."

"Something happen with Sally?"

"No, nothing to do with her. It's about a faculty member."

"Faculty member?"

"Have you heard the name, Michael McGibbon? I think I mentioned him to you before. He's new here. Came from Berkeley."

"So?"

"He'd been a lecturer at the Lutheran seminary. Heresay has it that the faculty pushed him out. We don't know why. The rumor is that he'd become too outspoken. Gay rights problem, we think. His wife divorced him."

"Go on."

"He's got a male partner who teaches at Harvey Mudd."

"What's the problem?"

"The faculty rules say teachers must live lives beyond reproach."

"Has he done something reproachable?"

Bill stammered, then said, "Not exactly, it's up to how you look at it."

"You know Bill, truth is in the eyes of the beholder. Depending on one's viewpoint, an action can be disgusting or harmless. The race for the White House is a case in point. A Bush-hater can't accept anything the President says, and people like Hannity on Fox News can pick out the tiniest speck on Kerry's lapel. Impartiality and independence are hard to hold on to. What's this professor's problem got to do with you?"

"Yesterday at school somebody posted a huge photo of the last Gay Pride Parade. McGibbon and his partner carried the banner. It was like their coming out party. The faculty is upset over what to do. Traditionalists demand that the prof be fired. They claim that if donors get wind of this, they'll cut off funding, maybe force the school to shut down."

"They couldn't do that, could they?"

"It's happened before. The Angela Davis controversy crippled the Presbyterian mission program. A vocal minority on the seminary board opposes the ordaining of homosexuals."

"Crisis in the making, you think. How can I help you?"

Bill didn't respond at first. He sounded as though he was consulting with some other persons. "Would you be willing to meet with a group of us? Guide us in working out a consensus."

"You flatter me. I'm not sure I can help, but...? I'd be willing to try. When and where?"

"A meeting on campus would be too obvious. I proposed our church. It's convenient and neutral. Saturday afternoon is best for us."

"I'll have to check on it and get back to you. Fireside room would be best."

"I really appreciate this. Sally may come, too. We need to report on our progress. Dr. Fergeson isn't charging me anything."

Joe followed the news closely as the California rhetoric over gay marriage got hotter every day. One East coast pundit accused Governor Schwarzenegger and Attorney General Lockyer of cowardice. He said they ought to arrest the San Francisco mayor.

Now the mayor is filing a lawsuit against the state for violating the California Constitution which outlaws discrimination.

Democrats can't agree on the issue, but most Republicans stand against same-sex unions. They're calling on the governor to enforce the law. Joe felt he had to stay one step removed from the fray. He hadn't made up his mind. He reasoned that if discrimination is wrong, then gays should have equal rights. But as some claim, if homosexual acts are sin, then the law must discriminate against it. With so much rancor over the law, Joe feared that the church might be sucked into a legalistic solution.

Oh, my God, help me discern the way. Give me your righteousness, seasoned with a grace that goes beyond our rights.

When Joe locked the car at church, he noticed his hand shaking. Taking several deep breaths, he headed toward the entrance. Bill and Sally met him on the patio.

"We're waiting here to direct the others," Bill said. "Should be at least a dozen coming. We really need you. Several guys demand that we boycott classes until the president disciplines the prof."

"I'll wait for you in the fireside room."

Three cars drove into the lot and unloaded an even mix of men and women. To Joe they looked like any other bunch of college kids. No one dressed alike. *These are our hope for tomorrow.* They filed into the room.

"Sit anywhere," Joe told them. "No speaker's table today."

"I think we're all here," Bill announced. "This is Rev. Weaver, a friend of mine here at Grace Alone. He has no ax to grind so should be evenhanded."

"Thank you, Bill. I'll try to be ambidextrous. Actually I feel like a basketball referee who can't please both sides. Where do we begin? Am I correct in understanding that you are agreed that you don't want your new professor and his partner to irreparably harm the school? What might that danger be?"

He looked around to see who was willing to answer. A tall athletic blonde fellow spoke up. "Some of us want to boycott his classes."

"That could backfire," another student said. "He might flunk us all."

"I have an idea," another fellow said, "a little weird perhaps. Could we persuade the people in his classes to pair up like same-sex couples. Hold hands as we enter class?"

"Humor would make our point," a supporter added. "It won't hurt anyone."

A female student objected. "Let's be straight forward. Go to the president's office and petition the school to warn the professor. Urge him to discipline McGibbon if he doesn't comply."

"Sounds like a UN resolution," a voice said to oppose.

Sally looked at Joe. "What do you think, Pastor Weaver?"

Joe stalled before answering. "First of all, whatever you do must not only be right but appear right. On such a delicate matter, subtle persuasion may be your best option. Publicity will defeat your purpose.

"Could we take each proposal and analyze it? Boycott suggests coercion, gaining reluctant submission.

"The humorous approach is what I would choose, but humor can cut deeply. It's easily misunderstood. If you resort to it, you'll need a spokesperson to explain the point in a sympathetic way.

"Petition might be effective, and you'd involve the administration on your side. That could be your safest course, but I can't tell you what to do. Even Jesus refused to judge on an inheritance issue between two brothers. He would want you to pray about it. The best solution will come from Him. End of sermon."

Bill Scully then took charge. "Let's take this advice, sleep on it and pray over it. Could we meet outside the dining hall after lunch on Monday? Shall we say one o'clock? Okay, see you then."

13
Waiting

Sunday morning Joe greeted Bill Scully in the coffee line but figured it wasn't the time or place to ask him how he expected the student meeting to turn out. Joe would have to wait, trusting the students to work out their own solution.

Yet, he couldn't keep from formulating his own opinion. Somewhere he had read about how important it was to put down in black and white one's own understanding of truth. If he could do that, there might come an opportunity to pass it on to someone else.

Joe believed in prayer, not to beg God to do what Joe wanted, but to commit matters to God as Jesus did in Gethsemane. "Let go and let God," he thought expressed it well.

After golf on Monday morning, he and his buddies from Eternally Young Retirement Community sat in the clubhouse eating sandwiches and drinking coffee.

Jake led off the conversation. "Have any of you seen Mel Gibson's *The Passion of the Christ*?

No one had, but Joe said he planned to see it. Based on some reviews, the others worried about excessive violence and possible anti-Semitism.

"Several of us," Jake said, "are planning a panel discussion. We need someone to present a positive viewpoint. He turned to Joe. "How about you?"

"Saa," he sighed in Japanese. "If I see it, I don't want to view it critically. I would go to be blessed. It would serve as a Lenten service for me, my own Gethsemane."

"I feel the same way," Homer said. "We discuss a topic to death, even when we can't do anything about it."

"It's hard to avoid becoming scattered," Joe said. "If I try to do too many things, I don't accomplish anything, except wear myself out."

"So," Jake said, "I'll take it that I have to find someone else for the panel."

Homer set his coffee down and said, "I'm done. Cleaning lady will be gone, so it's safe to go home. Everybody okay for Thursday?" They all nodded and headed out the door to the parking lot.

After they had loaded their clubs and gotten in the car, Joe turned to Jake. "Could I ask a favor of you? Some seminary students from the Upland seminary are meeting today to decide what they should do about a new professor who's flaunting his gay life style in public. Would you keep them in your prayers? Ringleader is Bill Scully from our church."

"I'll try to remember."

"I'm perturbed. They may ask me for advice. Why they think I'm an expert is beyond me."

The rest of the way back to Claremont, neither of the two said much. "Base Line is a lot more open and scenic than the 210," Joe said. "The 210 is like riding between two prison walls."

They turned down Mountain Avenue. As they passed Condit Elementary School, Joe said, "Wouldn't it be great to be a child again? Look at how carefree they are. Kids on a playground always cheer me up."

Jake didn't respond.

"You know, Jake, doesn't golf make you feel young again?"

"Ugh, if it weren't for my aching muscles. The heat really got to me today."

"See you at the prayer meeting," Joe said before lifting his clubs out of Jake's trunk. "It's my turn to drive on Thursday."

Joe heard Anita's piano playing as he approached the front door. It sounded to him like something loud and complicated from the *Elijah.*

Before going to the bedroom, he noticed a piece of paper on the floor. "What's this note?"

She stopped. "Katsunaga called. He'll be coming alone on Thursday afternoon. He wants to see the colleges and the Village."

"What time is he coming?"

"Three or three-thirty."

"Good, then we can check out that lecture at the seminary and maybe meet Bill Scully. They should get to know each other. They're about the same age."

Before walking to lunch, Joe glanced at the morning headlines but saw no new developments along the same-sex marriage battle front. After lunch, just as his eyes were closing for a nap, the phone rang.

"Bill Scully here."

"How'd your meeting with the students go?"

"Big crowd, maybe thirty of us. It took a while to work out a consensus."

"What did you decide?"

"We've settled on a two-pronged approach."

"What do you mean?"

"Tomorrow we're going to parade into class holding hands."

"I'd like to see that."

"The president will meet with us in the afternoon."

"Hope this works okay for you. Just don't antagonize people. A soft touch works best. "Oh, by the way, I've got somebody I want you to meet. He's the new pastor at the Japanese congregation in Yorba Linda. He's coming on Thursday. Could we meet you at the 4:30 lecture and then go out for supper?"

"Sounds good."

"Chinese okay?"

"I love Chinese."

"Would you bring the school catalogue. He might want to see what's offered."

"Will do. Thanks."

"See you on Thursday."

14
Emptiness

Wednesday night Joe felt uneasy about meeting Bill Scully and Shinichi Katsunaga. The storm over same-sex marriages unsettled him so that he no longer could feel secure in his own opinion.

That night he woke from a dream where he had entered a room with no furniture. "Why?" he said as he awoke. "Am I like an empty room, naked with no props to cling to?"

He crawled out of bed and turned off the alarm. In the dark, he tried to see what time it was. His inner clock suggested that it must be close to 5:00, so he walked down the hall to the living room. The TV clock read 4:50. He eased into his recliner to reflect about the meaning of his dream.

Was God telling him to clean up his life? "If you are to be of any use to others," God said, "you can only do it from a position of humility. Like Jesus you must empty yourself."

Joe turned on the lamp and reached for his prayer book. But even before he opened it, he realized God had told him that out of Joe's sinfulness would come the forgiveness that could clarify his vision.

He got up from the chair, walked to the front door, opened it and stepped out. He sucked in the cool air and immediately felt renewed within.

Later in the morning, his golf felt as stress-free as when he had won the Southern California Open, reciting, "*Iesu*, let it be."

During breakfast, disagreement about Mel Gibson's *The Passion of the Christ* didn't disturb him. Joe wasn't into nit-picking theological debate over Jesus' sacrifice. For him it was sufficient to believe that "God was in Christ reconciling the world to himself."

He had learned that through all the vicissitudes of life, a divine hand guided him. When a wall obstructed his path, God's hand would part a secret entrance for Joe to pass through. It seemed to him that from the high perspective of God, a way always could be found: through the wall, around it or over it. Today would be no different. Thursday, March 11, 2004 would reveal a path he had not seen before.

When he returned home, he showered and took a quick doze in his recliner before scanning the newspaper. He found nothing on the marriage issue. The UCLA cadaver scandal and the uproar over campus hate crimes reinforced his perception that greed and hate were well and thriving in California even among the elite.

By the time Joe read the daily mail after lunch, Katsunaga's car pulled up under the leaf-less walnut tree in front.

Not yet acclimated to the California informal dress code, Shinichi wore a navy-blue suit with a striped tie on a white shirt. "Come in," Joe said. "We have time for a cup of coffee. Lecture doesn't start until 4:30, but actually 4:40 student time."

Chitchatting about culture adjustments, shopping advice and news from the Japanese church, an hour sped by.

"*Shimatta*" (doggone it) Joe exclaimed. "I wanted to walk you through the Village before going to the lecture."

"No problem," Shinichi said. "I'll have other chances."

Joe began to take the coffee cups and cookie plate to the kitchen. He turned back to his guest. "Anita has *learned* me well." He laughed. "Does your wife keep you straight, too? I mean is she strict with you?"

"What do you mean?"

"Oh, nothing, but I've seen some of those dorm rooms at the Tokyo seminary."

Shinichi smiled. "You forget. My wife lived in the dorm, too."

Joe drove so that he could show off the Village, pointing out City Hall, the post office, specialty shops and favorite watering holes like the SomeCrust Bakery and Starbucks. He turned at 4th Street and drove by the huge congregational church to College Avenue, then straight north by the five colleges and the graduate university until at Foothill Boulevard, he turned right and headed east to Upland. At Central he went north until they reached the campus of the Theological Seminary of the West.

"I haven't been to any lectures lately. Can't go to everything. I tell people I'm busy being a full-time writer and part-time golfer."

"Writer?"

"Did one novel on Pastor Kiyoshi Watanabe's exploits in Hong Kong. My book *Golfing in Jesus' Spirit* just went on line — print on demand. Now I'm trying to figure out if and how to deduct expenses on my income tax."

"How old are you?"

"Seventy-nine, but I keep showing my drivers license to get senior discounts."

"Huh? I don't understand."

"Never mind. One of my old, stale jokes."

When they entered the lecture room, Joe counted about twenty guests, mostly outside clergy types and a few women plus five or six students, one of whom was Bill Scully, who now approached them.

"See you made it," Bill said.

"This is Pastor Shinichi Katsunaga."

"Glad to meet you," Shinichi said as he put out a stiff right hand accompanied by an awkward bow.

Bill drew closer to whisper into Joe's ear, "That's Dr. McGibbon over in front on the left. I'll tell you about him later."

They sat on the right in the back row. Joe said to Katsunaga, "The speaker is going to tell about Alfred North Whitehead. Have you heard of him? A British mathematician and metaphysicist who opened the door for new understandings about faith and science."

"I've heard his name. Someone at *Toshindai* Seminary (Tokyo Union Seminary) lectured about him once. I went, but didn't understand it."

"Well, we'll try again today." And try they did, but none of them grasped a word of what the guest lecturer said. Fortunately a local professor deciphered the erudition into plain English.

At the coffee break, while the three were standing near the display of books, McGibbon walked toward them. "Mr. Scully, is this Joseph Weaver from Grace Alone Church?"

"Yes, I am he. You must be Dr. McGibbon."

"The notorious Dr. McGibbon. I understand you've been meddling in seminary affairs."

Averting McGibbon's scowl, Joe turned to Shinichi. "This is our new Japanese pastor from Yorba Linda. He came along to get a taste of Whitehead."

"I had better excuse myself," Bill said. "I think I saw Sally in the hall." He went out but took a hard right to the men's room.

Wish I'd thought of that.

"So, the students are stirred up a bit, are they?" Joe asked.

Showing no discomfort, McGibbon said, "Modernity is in a time lag around here."

"Time lag?" Joe questioned, then he smothered the rest of his reply with overflowing kindness. "I'm trying to understand. If you'd be so kind, maybe we could discuss these matters in a more leisurely way. Let me give you my card." Joe reached into his wallet and pulled out a partially torn business card and handed it to the doctor, putting on the friendliest smile he could muster, he said, "I'm still in time lag. Excuse me, I think they're starting the question period."

15
Wisdom from Afar

After the lecture on the way to the restaurant, Joe turned on the radio to catch the six o'clock news. Train bombings in Madrid monopolized the news, but at the end the announcer reported that "The California High Court today halted gay marriages. By a unanimous decision the Supreme Court of California ordered San Francisco to stop marrying persons of the same sex. The Court will rule on the legality of the city's actions within the next few months. City officials as of 2:33 p.m. stopped issuing same-sex licenses."

"Finally!" Bill Scully sighed. "It took them long enough to make up their minds."

Shinichi Katsunaga didn't say anything, but after a few seconds asked, "What does that mean for the marriages of the couples already married?"

"I don't know," Joe replied. "They're probably in limbo."

"Limbo?"

"In doubt," Bill explained. "The word comes from the old Catholic belief about unbaptized babies — sort of halfway, neither in heaven nor hell."

"It will seem like hell to those who have tied the knot," Joe said. "I feel sorry for them. The restaurant is just ahead, a little beyond the supermarket."

Joe signaled to turn into the parking lot and soon found a space near the entrance. "Hope you both like this Chinese food. My wife and I are crazy about it."

They walked under the long canopy leading to the front entrance. Joe noticed that Bill picked up one of the take-out menus stacked inside the door and began perusing it.

"Could we have a quiet table?" Joe requested, and the hostess led them to a corner booth, near the doors to the banquet room.

No sooner had they sat down when a younger waitress came with glasses of ice water and a pot of tea. When the hostess spoke to the younger woman, Joe thought he recognized a Mandarin accent, but he wasn't sure. After Joe poured three cups of tea, the older lady came with three large menus.

"Any favorites for you?" Joe asked. "Why don't we each pick one dish and share? Okay? I know what I want, their special orange beef."

"Too many choices," Bill said. "I'll play it safe with sweet and sour pork."

Shinichi kept studying the menu, both the Chinese characters and the English.

"How about fish or chicken?" Joe asked.

"*Eeto* (let me think), maybe chicken with cashew nuts?"

"Good choice. My wife usually picks that one."

"I hear you might be interested in auditing a course?" Bill asked. "I brought a catalogue along for you to take home. He reached into his tote bag and handed it to Shinichi. Next time you come, we can talk about it."

"Bill, I couldn't help but notice that you sneaked away when McGibbon came over. Were you embarrassed?"

"Things are a little tense. He thinks I'm the ringleader."

"Well, aren't you?"

"We're all in it together. I just arranged for the meeting with you."

"When I met him, he didn't sound too antagonistic. I played it cool and tried to show sympathy, *sympathy* is the wrong word — *understanding* would be better. How'd your meeting with him go?"

A platter of orange beef appeared on the table, stopping the conversation. Bill, do you want to try chopsticks? We'll teach you."

"I'll stick to a fork."

"Tastes better with chopsticks."

After each one had taken a couple of helpings, Bill began to answer Joe's question. "It went quite smoothly, but…" Then, a platter of chicken and cashew nuts appeared on the table, and each one loaded some on his plate.

"Dr. McGibbon was ready for us. He…" The final plate of sweet and sour was squeezed onto the table, and they piled some of that onto their crowded plates along with scoops of rice.

"Go on," Joe urged Bill. "You talk; we'll eat."

"This is good food," Shinichi said. "That beef is *oishii naa.*" (very delicious)

"To continue, before we could present McGibbon with our petition, he began to read his own statement."

"Caught you by surprise, eh?"

"We were tongue-tied."

"What were his arguments," asked Joe.

"Please speak more slowly," Shinichi requested.

"McGibbon began by explaining his own homsexuality. By his tone it was clear that he'd been struggling a long while over it."

"What were his points?" Joe asked.

"He claimed that it is safest to have gays in monogamous relationships. If a gay tries to play straight, he could wreck a heterosexual marriage.

"They'd have shared possessions, giving stability. Also in time of illness, they would be more capable of making right medical decisions, better than relying on relatives who might not be emotionally stable enough to carry out a person's wishes. Also, he believes open persons are easier to integrate into congregational life.

"McGibbon summed up his thoughts by saying that he realized that God's ideal was marriage between a man and a woman. But circumstances must be considered."

"Were you able to talk about his points with him?"

"Not really. It was more like the opening statements in a court room. We were very uptight. He took the wind out of our sails by his reasoned opinions. I'm not sure he convinced any of us, but I give him credit for being frank with us."

Looking at Katsunaga, Joe said, "Sorry to throw this problem at you. You maybe can help us, but not now. Let's eat. They're bringing the ice cream and fortune cookies for dessert."

When they opened their fortune cookies, Bill exclaimed, "Hey, listen to this." Holding the paper up to the light, he read, "'Soon you shall receive wisdom from afar.'"

"How far?" Joe asked. Turning to Shinichi, he asked, "All the way from Japan?"

They laughed, then waited for Shinichi to read his. "It's too dark in here." Handing the paper to Bill, he asked him to read it.

"Oh, listen to this. 'I am more important than I realize.'"

"Ho, ho," Bill said. "We'd better listen to you. Hang on to this." Shinichi tucked it into his coat pocket.

"Okay, Pastor Weaver. What's your future? Out with it."

"Oh, for Pete's sake! 'Teaching you is like preaching to the Buddha — hopeless.' I'd better keep my mouth shut and listen to wisdom from afar." Looking at Shinichi, he said, "What can you tell us?"

"Eeto (let's see), can I say what I think?"

"Better than not thinking," Joe quipped back.

"All this commotion in the American church over sex, seems *mottainai."* How can I say that in English?"

"That's a tough one," Joe said as he shook his head. "Extravagant, wasteful to the point of impiety."

"Never mind. I shall say it differently. I think we Japanese Christians will not look kindly on this debate. Same-sex activity is taboo in Asia."

"Taboo?" Bill questioned.

"What seems strange to me is why should the American church decide such things? Is sex only an American problem?"

"It appears that way, doesn't it?" Joe said. "You may have a good point."

Bill looked deep in thought, then spoke, "Maybe I should ask some of the foreign students about it."

"Sounds like we've already begun to receive wisdom from afar," Joe said. "Of course, fortune cookies haven't made it into the biblical canon yet, but... we had better stop right there before I get heretical." They laughed as they left the table and made their way out to the car.

16
Descent to Hell

Imitating Howard Dean's internet promotion, the Gays and Lesbians for Evangelical Equality (GLEE) launched a campaign to promote their agenda. When Joe's wife checked the computer for messages on the 13th, she clicked on a new message titled "GLEE." Joe was sitting in the living room watching Robert Schuller interview a guest.

"Listen to this, Joe!" Anita called from the study. "GLEE's gone on the offensive."

"Print it out," he replied. "I want to watch this. Looks interesting."

When the cameras shifted to Schuller's son pitching for donations, Joe went to the study to get the read-out. He stood next to the printer and read aloud.

"Californians concerned about gender justice will rally March 20th at 2:00 p.m. in Ascension Lutheran Church, Pomona. The Reverend Rolf Konstanius, former bishop of Oregon, will speak on "It's About Time." Several gays and lesbians, including Dr. Michael McGibbon will share their testimonies. Volunteers will remain afterward to address envelopes for all delegates to the Synod's May Convention."

"They mean business. I'd like to go," Anita said.

"I should, too. Konstanius has quite a reputation as a spellbinder. I'd like to hear McGibbon. He's impressed the seminary students."

"The 20th is the first day of spring," Anita said. "Do you think they planned it to be a rite of spring?"

"Umm, interesting. God, I'll be glad when all this sex business gets settled. Did you see the article about the three school board members in Westminster objecting to letting pupils decide their own sex. Where's all this leading us?"

"Maybe we're too old for our time," Anita said.

"Back in Saijo, do you remember what Grandma Imao said when Nae-chan was born?"

"No."

"Wasurete kita." (forgot something), meaning born without a penis. Now can you have organ-less boys, and girls with male genitals. What next? I'm confused."

He moved over behind Anita and massaged her shoulders. Then he said, "No doubt about our babies. We left it for the doctors to announce, "You have a little girl or a little boy.""

"Oops, time for your favorite talk show, the McLaughlin Group."

"You know I can't stand John McLaughlin. How can you listen to him and that O'Reilly guy?"

"Abrasive, but they don't put you to sleep," he replied, as he returned to the living room. "Your favorite program is coming on after."

"What's that?"

"Keeping Up Appearances."

"You know I don't like that."

Joe called a family truce and turned on Tim Russert at 7:00.

Except for one telephone call from Bill Scully, the following week followed a regular routine. Bill reported that Sally and he were hitting it off well. Dr. Fergeson had proved to be very supportive. He'd helped Bill accept his sexuality, which he was learning was quite straight. He now knew he was a confirmed heterosexual.

That led Joe to feel safe to invite Bill to the GLEE Rally on the 20th.

"Do you think Sally might want to go with us, too?" he asked.

"Sally has heard about it from a lesbian student who is promoting it."

On Saturday, the 20th, Joe and Anita picked up Bill and Sally and drove them to the rally.

Ascension Lutheran Church stood in the middle of the block, just east of Garey Avenue. As they drew close to the church, they heard a raspy male voice haranging people. Entering the parking lot, directly in front of them hung a huge banner proclaiming:

"CONCORDIA DESCENDS TO HELL"

"Oh, for Pete's sake! That doesn't help anyone," Joe exclaimed.

"Who'll that persuade?" moaned Sally.

When the four of them got out of the car, two women wearing black armbands approached to hand them pamphlets denouncing homosexuality as the ultimate degradation. An Afro-American voice took over the microphone. It belonged to a tall round-collared preacher who pealed rolls and rolls of thunderous diatribes denouncing Hollywood and its degenerate culture that promoted gratuitous violence and ruderless sensuality.

"Anita, did you bring the cell phone?" Joe asked.

"Of course. Why?"

"Call 911 and ask the police to come. These nuts are disturbing the peace. There must be some limits to sound decibels. I'm going over and warn them."

"Be careful," Bill said.

"You and the women go in and save me a seat."

He walked over in front of the speaker and stood, motionless. The harangue continued as Joe stared relentlessly into the man's fiery eyes.

After several minutes, the speaker noticed Joe, giving him leave to come closer. Joe raised his hand to ask him to pause.

"Excuse me a second, could I have a word with you?"

"I'm busy, can't you see."

"Only a few seconds." Joe went up to the man and held out his hand, hoping for a response.

"You should know that someone has called the police. Maybe if you cut down the volume, they'll excuse you."

The big man looked puzzled, with an expression of unbelief. "This is a free country, isn't it?"

"Yes, but I think you're too loud. There's a law against too much noise."

In the distance Joe could hear a siren drawing closer. "They're coming. Just tone it down, then you'll be okay, I think."

"Suppose so. I've made my point anyway."

"I'm a minister, too," Joe told him. "No one wants a brother carted off to jail."

The police turned off the siren before coming into the parking lot. The cop got out and approached the speaker, but Joe headed him off.

"It's okay, officer. He's quieted down. I think he's a little deaf. He didn't realize how noisy he was."

The fellow with the gravel voice came running over to see what was happening. Joe held up his hand to stop him. "Everything's okay. No problem. These brothers got a little too enthusiastic," Joe explained to the officer. "They understand now."

"Good," the policeman said. "All is well that ends well." He looked over at the banner. "Who is this Concordia person going to hell?"

"Lutherans," Joe replied.

"My priest used to say the same thing, but more gently."

Joe laughed, but the two protesters weren't quite ready for humor.

"Thanks, officer." Turning to the other men and women surrounding them, Joe gave them a liturgical goodbye. "Go in peace."

The policeman looked surprised, then muttered back, "and serve the Lord."

17
The GLEE Rally

The church had plenty of empty pews. Joe spotted his three companions down toward the front and joined them.

"Did you get those hecklers quieted down?" Bill asked.

"I tipped them off that the police were coming. I bluffed by telling them the law forbade noise above a certain decibel."

"How'd you know that?" Anita asked.

"I didn't, but my bluff worked. I treated them like brothers. What does the program look like?"

"Starts off with a praise group from La Jolla. They're starting now," Bill said.

The lyrics were projected on a hanging screen. Joe didn't recognize any of the songs, but tried to sing along anyway, but Anita stayed seated and looked in pain.

The host pastor next welcomed everyone and plugged the GLEE movement as the cutting edge of the Lutheran Church. "We'll never be the same after the Synod convention. We are the 21st century reformers who will free the church from its Babylonian captivity to outworn traditions." Several Amens rose from the audience.

"Now I wish to introduce our newest member of the GLEE task force, the Reverend Dr. Michael McGibbon, Lutheran professor at our local seminary in Upland. We have invited him to share his testimony and vision for the future. Dr. McGibbon."

As he approached the pulpit, the pianist sounded the strains of "He's a Jolly Good Fellow," and some in the audience broke into song.

"Thank you, thank you, thank you," he began. First he described how he had been shunned in high school and never was able to be himself until he came out while teaching at the theological union in Berkeley. "I felt born again. My old stigmatized life style became my badge of honor. I wanted to help other gays and lesbians who were suffering in secret."

He went on to share several examples of students he had counseled. His last example told of how he had helped a very conservative minister see the light and accept his gay son.

"We must fight the good fight," McGibbon declared. "Sexual discrimination is the final barrier to conquer in our church and in our America." A group of enthusiastic students stood up and broke into loud applause and whistling. After two more testimonies, the M.C. announced, "Before we hear the keynote address from the Reverend Rolf Konstanius, retired bishop of Oregon, let us welcome The New Age Dancers."

To a jazzed up keyboard arrangement of "Bringing in the Sheaves," four pair of young women wearing white diaphanous angel costumes began a breezy interpretation of maidens bringing in the harvest. Gradually they closed in to form a tight circle around an imaginary soul and released it to the heavens.

As the dancers exited, the gray-haired bishop strode to the podium, faced the audience and screamed like a politician, "We shall overcome. Shout after me, we shall overcome. Again and again and again. Never give up. We shall win."

Joe turned to his wife, "He's out Teddy Kennedying Kennedy. This is more like a political convention or pep rally than a church meeting."

Konstansius then listed his platform for action.

1. Because God has created all persons equal, the church cannot justify the denying of homosexuals the right to be ordained into the ministry.

2. Since Jesus sent out the seventy, two-by-two, how can the church deny disciples today the chance to serve him in pairs?

3. In biblical times, the writers did not know that some persons were born with same-sex orientation. We know that God knows that, and God Almighty does not make mistakes.

4. We, too, must not declare unclean what God has created clean.

Then, one at a time he elaborated on his four points.

After he closed with prayer, the host pastor reminded everyone that after the meeting volunteers were needed to address and stuff envelopes with an appeal to delegates who would attend the Synod convention.

"Everybody stand as we close with "Stand Up, Stand Up for Jesus."

Joe noticed that Bill put his hand on Sally's knee and whispered in her ear. Joe would not have heard what he said except for the pause between stanzas. "Aren't you glad I'm not gay."

She smiled and pushed her head against his shoulder.

When they exited the church and greeted a few friends, they walked to the car. The protesters were still lurking around in front of the banner but no longer blasting over the loud speakers. They stood making the sign for shaming with their fingers. Then in unison they pointed their thumbs down and scowled, hissing the word *shame*.

After the four had buckled up in the car, Joe said, "I'm glad they didn't arrest them. The protesters are our brothers and sisters, too. I wonder if they'll show up at the Synod meeting. I know they can't be Lutherans — at least I hope not."

18
Beyond Integrity

The GLEE Rally upset Joe more than he had realized. It hadn't been so much what they had said, but the abrasive tone in which they said it. That night, Joe felt completely washed out. He was so tired that he didn't bother to watch his favorite talk shows. He stretched out on the couch and turned on TV to the Golf Channel.

He didn't even bother to fix a sandwich until 8 o'clock. Since his stomach was growling and queasy, he poured himself a glass of wine. About 9:00 he had to race to the bathroom.

Being a minimalist when it came to using medicine, he didn't take any right away. He returned to the sofa and listened to classical music thinking that might sooth him. Anita stayed in the study playing Free Cell on the computer. Finally she went to the kitchen and boiled an egg and made herself a peanut butter and jelly sandwich. She brought her supper in on a tray and squeezed in on the end of the sofa, forcing Joe to lift up his knees.

That triggered another dash to the bathroom. In a few minutes, he called to Anita, "Where have you hidden the Imodium?"

"Under my sink in back."

After downing a tablespoon of it, he returned to the living room and went to the recliner. "I don't feel so good," he complained.

"Hope you're not getting the flu."

"What a time to get sick." Joe remained there and tried watching the movie on PBS but soon fell asleep.

When Anita turned the TV off, Joe opened his eyes. "What time is it?" he asked.

"10:00."

"Guess I'd better go to bed. Tomorrow will be a busy day at church." Although he had slept almost an hour in the living room, he had no trouble falling back to sleep. Not even thoughts about the events of the day could keep him awake.

About 3:00, he went to the bathroom. When he returned to bed, he noticed that his head was hurting. "Hope I'm not coming down with a bug," he muttered to his wife.

In the morning he awoke about 7:00, got up and went to the living room. His sinuses were clogged, and he began coughing up phlegm.

Anita heard his hacking, so she came in to check on him.

"Sounds awful. You'd better stay home today."

"Do I feel hot?"

She placed her hand on his forehead. "Normal, I think. Should I get the thermometer?"

"Yeah, my joints ache."

She came back and put it into his mouth. After a minute, she held it close to the lamp. "Little high. I hope this isn't what's going around. They've quarantined the nursing home. I can't even go there to play my harp."

"Isn't it funny how God answers our prayers. On Friday when I was griping about being too busy, I asked God to help me ease up. He didn't answer as I would have liked. He lets me get sick so that I can't do anything. I can preach to myself about working at home, but it never works. I'm no good when I'm sick."

Anita looked him in the eye. "Maybe God is telling you something. If you're busy and fussing about all sorts of things, He can't get your attention. He speaks, but before the words reach you, you've moved on. Now He's got you."

"Do you think God says, 'I've gotcha now.'"?

"You'll probably be over this by the Kairos Board meeting on Friday."

"Oh, God, Friday and Saturday. I can't miss that."

"Who is vice-chairman?"

"We don't have one. I'll have to go, no matter what."

"This flu business is nothing to fool with."

"It's not SARS, anyway. Even the flu shot couldn't prevent it. It's a new strain, they say. I think we depend too much on medicine."

"The Imodium worked, didn't it?"

"That's true. This cold might only be an allergy. Winds have been pretty strong, and there are lots of trees in bloom." He sneezed hard, reached for some tissue and blew into it.

For four days Joe nursed his cold. He had wanted to go to Alhambra to talk over the issues on the agenda with the European Board members, but he had to rely on a few brief telephone conversations. When the day of the Board meeting arrived, Joe reached back into his memory bank to cash in on an inspiration he experienced fifty years before.

Joe had been down with a miserable cold. He was due to conduct a service in the Hoki home in Gota Village, six miles away. He was on the verge of canceling, when he recalled a healing account of Jesus. The record said that "the lepers were healed on the way." Could he once again trust God to "heal him on the way?" That time Joe did go, and by the time he stepped up into the Hoki home, he felt well and able to do the service.

When Friday arrived, Joe drove to the Board meeting twenty-six miles away. In spite of compulsive coughing that forced him to step out of the room several times, he stayed with it to the end, even remaining for the final dinner Saturday night. He'd been enabled to finish his responsibilities, witness the election of a Chinese business woman to replace him as chairperson and be feted by his colleagues.

That Saturday night driving home on the crowded freeway, he would have sung hymns of praise if he hadn't had such a raw throat and stuffy nose. He thanked God for helping him and releasing him from the chairmanship. Now he was primed for full-time concentration on the church's struggle over homosexuality. He didn't know how he could help, but he believed that somehow God would make a way beyond his and everyone else's understanding.

19
Stripped Bare

Joe had persevered, but the coughing persisted. It became so annoying that the dining room staff ordered him to stay away. For more than a week, it was virtual house arrest. He was shunned and forced to eat from a dinner tray delivered to the house. By Palm Sunday, April 14, he had become well enough to attend church. Instead of carrying a palm branch with others, he slipped into the sanctuary and took a seat near the front. Along with a handful of disabled and elderly parishioners, he didn't get up for the singing and Gospel lesson. Several of his golf buddies stared at him with sympathy. During the passing of the peace, one of his friends offered to help him stand up, but Joe declined.

Afterward at coffee time, he stayed seated and let others come to him. He had heard people before say how hard it was to receive care from others. That proved especially true for an extrovert like Joe Weaver. He was not accustomed to feeling handicapped. He wanted to do for others rather than have them do for him.

During the first three days of Holy Week, he lay low at home, but on Maundy Thursday, he and Anita went to the Communion Service. At the very end, the pastor with the help of the acolytes and altar guild, began stripping the altar and pulpit of the paraments, fair linen, candles and cross. The symbolic implications of this laying the church bare spoke to Joe's heart. He could not shake off the visual image of the beautiful church deprived of all ornamentation. The memory stayed with him till bedtime. He remembered the experience of Job in the Old Testament, "a man whom no other person could excel in faithfulness and goodness." Yet, God permitted him to lose everything. He was stripped of his wife, children and possessions. He lost everything he had worked for.

If I lost everything, would I be able to survive?

Joe Weaver fell into a deep sleep. He dreamed a dream he could never forget. It mirrored the peak in his career when the media center in Tokyo was celebrated in the ballroom of the Nikkatsu Hotel. In the dream he inaugurated the re-opening of the center, but it unfolded differently from the original event. This time the center contained no furniture. He recognized familiar faces from the press corps and churches, but there were no bouquets or decorations. "Why?" he uttered as he stirred into wakefulness.

He expected Jesus to answer him at once, but God's reply shocked Joe to say, "Not that answer?" In an instant of enlightenment, he realized that he would have to clean out all self-righteousness from his heart. Like Job, Joe Weaver had believed in his own integrity. For thirty-eight chapters Job had defended his own righteousness, but in the end God himself confronted him. Out of the storm, the Lord spoke to Job. "Who are you to question my wisdom with your empty words? Stand up straight. Answer the questions I ask you."

For a brief moment, every one of God's accusations against Job pummeled Joe Weaver, grinding him down to nothingness.

"Joe, you challenged Almighty God; will you give up now, or will you answer?"

Drained of everything, good and bad, Joe dared to look up and address his Maker: "I spoke and thought foolishly, Lord. What can I answer? I will not say anything. I have already said more than I should."

An eery silence pervaded the air, like the fearful stillness in the eye of a hurricane, the world stopped. Joe gasped, breathless. His lips moved, but no words came out. Helpless to put his nothingness into speech, he flung himself before the blinding light of God's presence. Next he saw that a hand reached down out of the light to lift him to his feet. From swirling smoke surrounding the light, flew a burning coal that touched Joe's lips. The red-hot ember whispered to him, "Now your guilt is gone, and your sins forgiven."

Not knowing how to reply, he was unsure of how to accept this strange message of pardon.

Finally he made Job's words his own: "In the past I knew only what others told me, but now I have seen with my own eyes. I am ashamed of all I have said and repent in dust and ashes."

20
Resurrection

On Easter morning, the risen Christ lifted Joe out of his despondency. He knew he had been rebirthed for some purpose. "Jesus, your will be done," he prayed. With fresh confidence, he believed God would give him the insights and the courage to prevail in the coming storms.

Joe kept hearing news that there were congregations on the verge of splitting, church councils threatening to resign, and protest letters fired off to Concordia Church headquarters in Milwaukee. The media also reported troubles in other denominations. Several heresy trials had ended in deadlock. When congregations tried to order the study books on sexuality, they were told that they were sold out.

The Southern California Synod convention was coming in five weeks. Joe worried about what might happen if GLEE and its opponents in the Family Values Coalition clashed in debate. So far, he had heard of no viable middle-of-the-road voices arising to mediate the extremes.

Then like a bomb, the *Los Angeles Chronicle* ran a story on April 14th with the headline: Lutherans Defy Their Doctrines. Renegade Churches To Call Active Homosexuals. "The storm has hit," Joe exclaimed when he saw the article. He hurried to show it to Anita. "They're repeating what that church in the Bay area did.

"I feel sorry for Bishop Friberg. He's compelled to enforce discipline. He'll have to sever synodical ties to that church."

"What's the Lutheran doctrine they're defying?" his wife asked.

"I don't know. I can't recall anything in the confessional writings. I believe the Reformation theologians simply assumed marriage was between a man and a woman. What's disturbing about this headline is that the public now will perceive that the church is flouting its own teachings. Even if it's not true, people will think it's true. We can't recuse ourselves from this challenge." He walked over and plopped himself in his wife's easy chair and sat thinking.

"If my memory is right, back in the '70s the Lutheran World Federation faced a similar dilemma."

"I don't remember that," Anita said.

"It was on another issue. The German-speaking congregations in the Namibia area of South Africa hadn't integrated their congregations."

"What happened?"

"The debate revolved around a Latin phrase, *status confessionis*, which means the status of faith. If it were deemed a doctrinal issue, the LWF would have to expel them."

"Label them heretical?"

"They did reach a temporary solution by suspending those churches from membership until they accepted blacks."

"Is the *Chronicle* saying same-sex marriage denies church doctrine?" Anita asked.

"Won't the public see it as such?"

"Did you see that the Vatican might deny communion to John Kerry over abortion? He should stay out of that fray," Anita said.

"And be labeled a coward? God, I wouldn't want to be a bishop these days...."

"Coward," she chided with a smile.

"We should imitate the Brits and pray 'God save the President — and us all.'"

21
Death to Life

On the first Sunday of May, a guest by the name of Frederick Dussenberg preached at Grace Alone Church. He had been a classmate of the pastor's father in seminary. For the past thirty-five years he had served in the Beirut Christian Center. He was fluent in Arabic and familiar with Middle East customs. He began his sermon like this:

"You may be surprised that your pastor did not invite me here. I asked him if I could come. Two years ago Muslim radicals launched a series of verbal attacks against our center. They claimed that our work for reconciliation between Muslims and Christians threatened Islam. They roughed up some of our staff and intimidated people coming to the center. About that time, a friend sent me a copy of *Pre-emptive Love* written by one of your members. He had worked with Pastor Kiyoshi Watanabe in Hiroshima after World War II. By any chance is Mr. Olson here today? Or, should I ask if Joe Weaver and his wife Anita are here today?"

Joe, who was seated next to the center aisle, raised his hand. He pointed toward the choir. "My wife is hiding over there behind the organ."

"The book," Dussenberg continued, "could not have arrived at a better time. We were about to shut down the work, but a little voice inside me said, 'Read the book your friend sent.' I also recalled that back in 1970, I was a guest at the Weavers' home in Tokyo. That very night I began reading after supper and didn't stop until the early hours of the morning. The example of Pastor Watanabe's heroic deeds to save the dying prisoners in Hong Kong spoke like Jesus himself to me. His story touched our hearts in 2002. Like Watanabe we knew that 'We must obey God rather than men.' The concept of pre-emptive love grabbed hold of us. We no longer quivered behind locked doors like the first apostles. We went out to our enemies. We told them that we considered them our brothers. If we had wronged them, they should tell us how so that we might ask for forgiveness.

"I recalled how St. Francis of Asissi had crossed the no man's land between enemy armies. We gave them copies of St. Francis' prayer for peace, asking them to study it. If they desired, would they pray it with us?

"Two or three days later, Mohammed Salif, their leader, visited our center. Although the room was conspicuously Christian with a large crucifix on the wall, it did not provoke Mohammed. After we sat down and offered him good strong coffee, he said to us, 'We Muslims consider Jesus a prophet.' He motioned with his head toward the crucifix, then added 'but we can never believe that he arose from the dead. You came and offered your hand of friendship, pleading for us to show what sins against us you could confess. Something mysterious happened. For a brief moment, I doubted that Jesus remained dead. You appeared like people who believed that He still lived. That's why you dared approach us. You made us feel like friends. Now, if it will not offend you, allow me to embrace you.' With beard and all he did just that and even kissed me.

"I have come here to thank you," the preacher continued. "I want you to visualize my text like a movie. The camera is panning the scene from a distance. We see a procession of people carrying a coffin from a city. Down at the right Jesus is walking along, followed by twelve men, many women and children. The two groups are on a collision course. Jesus raises his hand to halt the funeral column. It looks as though he is talking with the pallbearers and a woman who is weeping. He touches the coffin. The corpse sits up. We hear shouts of "Hallelujah!" The two processions merge, going away from the burial site of death and back to a city called Nain.

"That is what we experienced in Beirut. Jesus had imbued us with life so that we could become one with those who had been servants of death.

"You also must go and do likewise. Obey God rather than men. Seek out your enemies in love. Ask God to show you how. He will answer quickly, but often not as we expect. His ways transcend our ways. Amen."

The sermon left Joe numb. If he were to intercede in the church's impending conflict, what should he do? Pastor Dussenberg said, "Pray." But how? Before his mind had uttered the word *how*, Joe found himself resorting to his old golfing prayer: "*Iesu* (Jesus), let it be." He knew he had to follow Jesus in a spiritual death. As in Mel Gibson's movie, the full moon of God's presence over the Garden of Gethsemane guaranteed that the Lord would orchestrate events to fulfill his will.

Resembling a novelist who knows the eventual outcome of a story, he cannot know in advance the many stops and turns that must be navigated before reaching the final destination. That insight gave Joe enough to go on. Like Abraham, he believed God was calling him down an unknown road that only He knew. He would lead to whatever goal He desired.

22
Sunday at Yorba Linda

After church, Bill Scully ran up to Joe and exclaimed, "Wasn't that sermon great? It really hit home."

"All we have to do now is follow God's road map," Joe replied. "The trouble is He'll only turn one page at a time. As with map books, it's easy to miss the way when a new page is needed. Let's get our coffee and go over to the bench to see if we can figure out which page we're on."

Bill stacked his napkin with a homemade oatmeal cookie, one fudge bar and a bunch of grapes. Then with the right hand he took a coffee cup and joined Joe who had been content with only an Oreo cookie and coffee.

"Everything okay with Sally?" he asked. "Any problems with Dr. McGibbon?"

"Fine with Sally, but I've heard that McGibbon and some friends are going to push a resolution at the Synod Convention."

"So, he's following through. I suspected that when we heard him at the GLEE Rally."

"What should I be doing?"

"You heard what Dussenberg said. Maybe what they did in Beirut could be our way. What do you think, Bill?"

"The professor isn't our enemy. Would it help if I went to some of McGibbon's planning sessions with other students?"

"Not as a spy, for goodness sake."

"No, as a potential sympathizer. How would that be?"

"If you're comfortable with it. What about Sally? Can she get close to the girls? There were quite a few at Ascension that day."

Bill paused to think, then said, "I can ask her. It would look natural. We're always together anyway. They're going to want some heterosexuals on their side. By the way, has Katsunaga contacted you since we met last?"

"No. I assumed he was busy with Lent. I need to call him. He might be the key to finding a middle way in the dispute. Japanese are very good at finding common ground. They don't like confrontation. They had too much of that in the '30s. I'll give him a call."

"Why don't we visit him? We owe him one."

"He'd like that. Then we can see his church. What time is it now? His service should be over. Japanese services always start at 10:30. They'll be eating the usual curry rice about now. Let's call him."

Joe spied Anita coming out of church and called to her. "Let me borrow the cell phone." She came over and handed it to him. Scrutinizing its face, he asked, "Where do I punch it on?"

"The green spot."

"See if I do this right." Pulling out the aerial, he reached into his black tote bag and removed his datebook. Finding Shinichi's number, he cautiously punched in the numbers.

"Moshi, moshi, Sei Paoru Kyokai (Hello, this is St. Paul Church), a woman's voice said.

"Is Pastor Katsunaga there? May I speak with him?" The woman understood and went to call him, *"Katsunaga Sensei, odenwa desu."*

"Hello, this is Reverend Katsunaga."

"Joe Weaver here. Sorry to interrupt your lunch. Curry rice, I suppose."

"No curry today. We eat *udon* (noodles) on the first Sunday of the month."

"I'm here with Bill Scully. Could we see you next Sunday? We'd like to worship at your church. After lunch, could we do some more talking about the Synod meeting?"

"No problem. We'd love to have you. I'll mail you the directions."

"That went well. He sounded honored that we're going there. You can get a taste of Japanese worship. I wonder how much it's been Americanized."

Sunday, May 9th coincided with Mothers' Day. When Bill and Joe entered the church, an elderly lady in kimono greeted them at the door and pinned a red carnation on Bill and a white one on Joe. She bowed low and motioned with her hand toward the opening to the sanctuary. As in most Japanese churches, behind her against the wall stood a wooden stand with many cubbyholes with members' names written underneath. A dark wooden table faced the entry way. It was stacked with hymn and liturgy books, Bibles, bulletins and a guest book.

"Would you please sign your name here," the greeter said.

Bill looked puzzled. "Every church does this," Joe explained. "Then they'll know whom to contact." After signing in, a woman usher led them toward the front.

When they had seated themselves, Joe whispered to Bill, "We still don't allow women ushers at Grace Alone."

"How come?"

"Tradition. The men think they keep things more dignified than women."

"Sally should see this."

The organist began playing on the electric Yamaha. Pastor Katsunaga came out of the sacristy robed in white with a green stole. He proceeded to the altar, paused to bow in prayer, then turned to face the congregation. Nodding a welcome to Joe and Bill, he announced the opening hymn. Everyone stood to sing.

In Shinichi's sermon, he occasionally inserted some English for the young people in attendance. At the end, he explained why Bill and Joe had come.

After the sermon, Katsunaga gave an explanation for their presence: "Our church in America is divided over the issue of ordaining practicing homosexuals and over whether to allow ministers to bless same-sex unions. Mr. Scully, a student at the seminary in Upland, and retired missionary Pastor Weaver are here to consult with me about what we should do at the Synod Assembly. I think we may be able to help the American church."

"Whew!" Joe sighed. "That fortune cookie could be right. 'Wisdom from afar' might be coming."

The curry served was not as hot as the Indian version, but not as bland as what the Eternally Young cooks offered up. Bill pretended to listen while Joe made Japanese conversation with a gentleman who had been born in Hiroshima but immigrated to the U.S. in the early '50s.

"I'm glad you two could talk," Shinichi interrupted and looking at Joe said, "would you mind joining me in the sacristy? I've got some ideas about the Assembly." He closed the door behind him tight. Shinichi moved behind his desk. Bill and Joe pulled up chairs in front of him. "What have you got in mind?" Joe asked.

"Can we find a way to use pre-emptive love? I'm a voting delegate, right?"

"I only have the privilege of the floor," Joe said, "but I'm working to get our church president to appoint Bill one of our lay delegates. Then Shinichi can make a proposal which Bill seconds. I step to the mike and make a plea to pass it, but what should the motion be?"

"I understand you," Shinichi began. "but hadn't I better discuss this with the other foreign-language ethnic pastors? We're meeting in Santa Barbara this week. It would be stronger if all of the ethnic ministers made the proposal. I'm not sure they would want a Japanese representing them."

"I get you," Joe nodded in consent, then paused in thought. "Bill, you might want to interview foreign students at school." He noticed Shinichi glancing at his watch. "It's time Bill and I be going." He caught Bill's eye and said, "Sally will be waiting for you."

"Thanks for coming. I'll let you know what I find out from the other pastors."

Joe took a business card from his pocket. "Let me give you our wireless phone number. We'll be down at the beach near San Diego this week. Call when you find out something."

"Your actions don't affect only Americans."

"Yeah," Bill said. "The Episcopal Church is finding that out. Churches in Southeast Asia and Africa have broken ties with them."

"I don't think the Japanese will do that," Shinichi said. "They'll keep quiet, but complain behind your back and gradually send your missionaries home. They'll lose confidence in you. I don't want that to happen. I'm new here. But next week at the ethnic-church pastors' retreat, I'll see what I can find out. There are twelve different language churches."

"Good. Bill, you might interview foreign students at the school," Joe said. He noticed Shinichi again looking at his watch. "It's time Bill and I should be going." He caught Bill's eye and reminded him, "Sally is waiting for you."

"I'll let you know. Thanks for coming. It meant a lot to us."

23
Uncertain Certainty

The next afternoon, the uncertainty of life overwhelmed Joe's spirit as he and Anita drew near Oceanside. Traffic barely moved. Because of many police and squad cars along the road, they surmised that something special must be happening.

"Isn't Camp Pendleton next to Oceanside?" Anita asked.

"Maybe so. That could explain the extra security and all the flags. Maybe people are welcoming troops home from Iraq."

"Or sending them off. Let's stop at that Arco station."

Joe flipped on the right-turn signal, moved into the next lane and pulled into the gas station. "I'll fill the tank while you find out what's happening."

While he waited for the tank to fill, he asked the man at the next pump, "What's all the security for?"

"Marines are back from Iraq. That's why there are so many flags."

The gas nozzle clicked off. Anita returned to the car. "It's a parade," she announced. "The Marines are marching. The way is blocked. We'll have to go by way of Carlsbad and backtrack. Take a left ahead at the light." With the help of Anita's navigating, Joe avoided the parade and ended up driving north to reach their timeshare.

After checking in, they loaded a dolly with luggage and proceeded to their room. Joe turned on the TV. The first channel to light up was the local one, telecasting the parade live. Marines, six abreast, marched past the cameras. Flag-waving patriots lined the parade route. Close-up shots caught women weeping for joy to see their men home. One woman, with a baby hanging on her stomach and holding two little girls, wept profusely.

"Ani, come here. Look at the lady with those kids. What a homecoming their daddy will have tonight!"

"Some wives won't be so lucky," she snapped back. "Why must we send them over there to suffer and die?"

Joe kept still. He knew it was no time to argue over why. The two of them sat on the couch and watched what seemed like an endless procession of America's finest.

"Would you bring the bags in?" Anita asked. "I'll put the food away."

When they had settled in, Joe went to the kitchen and put on the coffeemaker. "I didn't dare drink any before we left. Why can't California have more rest stops along the way?"

Before the coffee was ready, Anita took out her phone to call the Johnsons in San Diego, but couldn't get through. She stepped out on the balcony to try again. Joe couldn't hear from inside, but by his wife's animated expression, he could tell that she and Marty Johnson must be plotting a bird trip.

"It's all set for Wednesday," Anita said as she came inside. "Carl will get a tee-time for you two. We'll meet for supper. They know a good Mexican restaurant in Carlsbad."

"Tomorrow is free then? I can do some writing. I need to organize my notes and see if I can get over my writer's block. This seaside view should help. Too much of my novel has been happening in Claremont."

After sleeping till 7:30 the next morning, he went out on the balcony, breathed in the salt air and prayed that ideas would roll in like the huge waves pounding the beach.

The psalm for the day was 66. He asked God to give him a special verse for the day. Reading swiftly, he came to verse 9 and stopped because it was underlined. "He has kept us alive and has not allowed us to fall." He tried to remember what he was doing when he had underlined that verse, but gave up and let the words be his inspiration for the day. Opening his devotional booklet, the lesson stressed that "God will baptize you with the Holy Spirit and fire." He wondered if the Lord had preserved his life this long for some special purpose. He always had believed and taught that everyone has a unique niche in life. *Niche* could mean being pigeonholed. Joe didn't believe that God would do that. But he might work his purposes in spite of our inaction.

That triggered a memory of Walter Trobisch, the German exchange student who had survived the Battle of the Bulge. Now, Joe thought, our forces in Iraq face a similar crisis in the battle for Fallouja. His thoughts went back to the day when Trobisch had preached. Joe never forgot that Walter said, "A Christian is someone who can wait." From his own experience, Walter had to wait a long time for his wife-to-be, Ingrid Hult. "We need not fret," he explained. "God in his own good time will fulfill His purposes, with or without our help."

God, save the men and women in Iraq. Save our President and leaders of all countries. You can save us. Show us and our people the way.

He flicked on the TV to CNN's Breaking News from somewhere near Fallouja. "Today four soldiers received baptism in a portable font," the announcer said. "Their comrades emptied water from canteens so that there was enough for the ceremony."

He pushed the mute button, then said to his wife, "If only we all could be washed clean.

"God," he prayed aloud, "give our whole nation a new birth of freedom, a revived sense of hope for ourselves and our enemies. Make us a people of kindness — even in the midst of war."

The cell phone rang, interrupting his prayer. "Is that our phone tune?"

Anita hurried to answer it. "Hello, hello. Yes, this is Mrs. Weaver. My husband. Hold on. I'll get him. It sounds like Katsunaga."

Joe took the phone. "Katsunaga Sensei? Good thing I gave you this number. What's happening?" Joe walked over to the other side of the room for clearer reception.

"You've already talked about homosexuality? Wait a second. I want to write this down." He picked up a pad from the coffee table and started taking notes.

"What's he saying?"

"Quiet, I can't hear."

"Lots of wisdom from afar. It's a good thing you talked it over with them. Great! We'll have to talk again before Synod. Thanks for calling." Joe set the phone down on the table and faced his wife.

"Well, what did he say?"

"Sungdo Kim didn't like the idea of a Japanese making the motion. Shinichi felt bad about it. The good news is that the whole group agreed to formulate a resolution. They want to stand together when it's presented at Synod. We'll meet at 11:00 the day the Assembly begins.

24
The Humbling

One week before the Synod gathering, Shinichi Katsunaga telephoned Joe at home. He sounded apologetic. He explained that the ethnic pastors had not endorsed Joe and Shinichi's strategy.

"I am sorry it didn't work out as you hoped," he said.

"Did you find out what their objection was?"

"It may have been a problem of language. A lot gets lost in translation because we're not used to dealing with sensitive issues in English."

"I can understand that. I recall meetings where the Filipinos and Indians dominated the talk. The Japanese and Koreans felt intimidated. One of my Japanese friends compared his feelings to charging a battery. By the time he'd get charged with enough courage to speak up, the agenda had moved on."

"I'd never heard that battery comparison before, but I think it's what I experienced in the meeting."

Joe sat down. "Where do we go from here?"

"We appointed Sungdo Kim, Wilbur Chan from Hong Kong and Isaiah Menkir from Ethiopia to draw up a draft resolution. On the morning of the Assembly, we are to meet in the hotel lobby at 11:00 to finalize the wording and decide how to present it."

"Why those three men?"

"I suppose because they talked the most, and they're good in English. I was surprised to find out that they did not want me to be one of the spokesmen."

"How come?"

"No one said it outright, but I could sense a resentment against a Japanese doing it."

"None of them were living during the Pacific War," Joe said. "It's hard to believe that the second generation still has it in for Japanese. Why the Ethiopian?"

"They've had a grudge against the Italians who invaded their country in the 1930s. He said it was time to forget the past. Everyone felt Chan would be the best spokesman."

"Why was Kim included?"

"He had strong feelings about the issue, even though his English isn't too easy to understand. He wants something said about divorce, too."

"This could be interesting," Joe responded, "seeing that several divorced pastors are in our Synod."

"Do you think any of the group will object if I sit in on your meeting?"

"No, in fact, they urged me to tell you to come."

"That's all well and good, but I think I'll lay low and not speak too much. Anything else?"

"Just come on the 20th. See you there. *Sayonara*."

Not being able to study a draft proposal worried Joe. He never liked to face surprises. He'd had bad experiences in college debates when he had to rebut someone. He never was quite sure of what to say or how to say it. Then when he'd said it, he feared he'd garbled his arguments. He was much more comfortable giving a canned speech, even if it sounded memorized.

To organize his thoughts, Joe drafted his own personal proposal but kept it to himself. From long experience in Japan, he knew it would be self-defeating to give copies of his ideas to the ethnic pastors. Any resolution they formulated would have to be their own, not like the so-called MacArthur constitution the Japanese adopted after World War II. Better to ask questions that will help the others see any blindspots and words that could be misunderstood.

With this resolve, Joe Weaver prepared his heart to interact with the ethnic brothers and one sister from Vietnam. On the morning of May 20th, he arose early and spent more time than usual in meditation. Because the Ontario Red Roof Inn was only five miles away, he golfed as usual at Marshall Canyon with his buddies and ate breakfast with them. He arrived home by 9:30, with ample time to clean up and head for the Assembly site.

Arriving in the hotel lobby at 10:45 he found the others sitting at the far end of the lobby. He spied Shinichi, who motioned for Joe to come sit in the chair next to him. Joe didn't recognize the others, except for Wilbur Chan, whom he had met before in Hong Kong.

Pastor Chan stood up to make an announcement. "The hotel frowns on meetings in the lobby; so Bishop Friberg has arranged for us to meet in the Rose Room. Let's proceed there and get started."

True to its name, the walls of the room were covered with frescoes of roses. The table around which the chairs were set featured a bouquet of many colored roses as the centerpiece. Chan waited for stragglers but called the meeting to order at 11:05. "We think that our resolution should be short and straight to the point. Pastor Menkir, would you read the proposal after everyone receives a copy. He waited while they distributed the paper. Have you all got a copy now?"

Menkir cleared his throat, then began to read. "We, the pastors of ethnic churches in the Synod, urge that the Concordia Lutheran Church, USA, avoid acting unilaterally on issues concerning sexuality. We believe the CLC should inform sister churches overseas and ecumenical partners of any proposed changes in the regulations regarding the marriage and the ordination of homosexuals. Furthermore, in the light of the increasing divorce rate, we recommend that the counseling offered to candidates for marriage be strengthened. We believe any laxity by our churches on these matters borders on a repudiation of natural law and the scriptural traditions of the universal church. We implore the CLC to consult with sister churches and report their reactions back to the Council of Bishops for consideration before the national church votes to make any changes in the present policies."

"Pastor Kim, you wish to speak?"

"Our committee moves that we accept this statement as our basic thinking and present it to our Southern California Synod."

"I call for the vote!" someone shouted.

"Okay? Chan asked. "All in favor raise your right hand. It looks unanimous. That was easy. Thanks for your cooperation."

25
Waiting Is Hard

Joe remained seated until everyone had left the Rose Room. He didn't want to be noticed as part of the ethnic caucus, lest other delegates accuse him of influencing their deliberations. But when he went through the doorway, Bill Scully and Sally Ryan were there waiting for him.

"We need to talk," Bill said. "This morning we bumped into Dr. McGibbon by the book displays. He said he had hoped to see us before opening worship."

"What did he want?"

"One of his former students, a man from Korea, told him about what the ethnics were planning."

"Was it Kim?"

"He didn't say, but he implied that the man felt very uneasy about trying to influence the U.S. church."

"I see," Joe said. "Did he say anything specific?"

"Only that as a Korean citizen, he didn't feel qualified to exert pressure on the church which has been so generous to him."

"It's funny he didn't speak up at our meeting today. We should have made certain that all voiced their opinions."

"McGibbon didn't actually say it, but he hinted to him that GLEE might be offering a pro-gay/lesbian resolution."

"That's how I understood it," Sally said.

"I think we should assume that. As long as the ethnic resolution gets approval, it won't make any difference what Synod does on GLEE's move."

"How so?" Sally asked.

"This is a national church issue, so synods can only present petitions to the whole church. It affects the entire church, sort of like civil rights in the U.S. You can't have each synod acting like an autonomous state."

"Are you saying that it resembles what the states are struggling over?"

"Shouldn't it be obvious?" Bill said. "That's what has upset so many people. If Massachusetts accepts gay marriages and others states don't, there'll be endless litigation."

"Why don't we go get some coffee and sit down," Joe proposed.

As they approched the Lutheran Social Services booth, Joe recognized Glenn Sanderson, a retired pastor, doing the serving. "LSS is always serving," Joe explained to Sally loud enough for Sanderson to hear.

"Coffee is the Swedish gasoline that runs the church," he quipped back.

"How about a donut? Thrivent Financial supplies them free to delegates."

"Okay. Let's put our investments to good use."

Taking their coffee and donuts over to an empty table in the corner, Joe saw Dr. McGibbon approaching them. "Here comes Dr. McGibbon."

"May I join you?" he asked.

"Grab a chair," Joe said. "Free coffee and donuts are over there."

"No thanks. I've got to watch my weight."

"Don't we all," Joe said, but then added, "Sorry, not you, Sally."

"Delegates, attention please," came a disruptive woman's voice over the public address speakers. "Lunch boxes can be picked up near the registration desk."

Moving his chair closer, McGibbon asked with a tinge of gruffness, "Do you know what the ethnic delegates are up to?"

Bill and Sally looked at Joe.

"I think they're trying to put their two cents into the homosexual discussion," Joe replied. "Are they trying to imitate the Methodists and Anglicans?" Sally asked. "Their overseas partners are blocking gay rights."

"That's one way of describing it, but hardly accurate." Joe tried to explain. "Lutherans are much more cautious, less apt to ride on a bandwagon.

"You've heard of the task force of theologians commissioned to study the problem? They're trying to ferret out the biblical issues so that the congregations and their members can study what's involved."

"I know that. What's so diffficult to figure out?" McGibbon asked. "If we don't come into the twenty-first century, the world will pass us by. It's only a matter of time before all the mainline Protestants declare themselves 'open and affirming churches.'"

"I'm not so sure Lutherans will march in step with the others," Bill said. "From what I hear, even among younger people, our Concordia members are more apt to take a stand against the trend. One of my classmates who attended a meeting of pastors said the speaker told of a prominent Lutheran leader who said that he always had been inclined to get on board the ecumenical ship. Figuratively speaking, he said as he was about to go up the gangplank, he looked up and read the name of the ship: SS Titanic."

Sally and Joe laughed, but McGibbon did not.

"A humorous story," Joe said, "but there are quite a few people in the pews who agree."

"So, what's your point?" McGibbon frowned back at Joe.

"Maybe we should all lighten up. Nothing will be permanently decided by the Southeran California Synod. Everything we recommend must go to the national church Assembly. Whatever the ethnics propose won't become the rules of Concordia until the General Assembly in August."

"It's easy for you to say that. For us gays and lesbians, we've waited too long already."

"Nothing is as hard as waiting. The Good Book tells us over and over that the Christian must wait on the Lord."

"I know, I know, but it is so hard to do."

With that note of finality, he excused himself and meandered among the book displays, pretending to examine the titles, but more than likely, Joe thought, puzzled by their conversation.

26

A Passover

On the drive home after the Synod's evening session, no one spoke until the car safely entered the freeway.

Sally broke the silence. "It was a great thrill for me today. I can't remember when I've heard such singing. I heard someone in the lobby ask the desk clerk if the Mormon Tabernacle Choir was in town."

"We're famous for singing. Garrison Keilor often speaks about it," Bill said.

"Another thing I noticed — people hugging each other, just like a family reunion. When the Synod Treasurer got up to propose that the convention go to biennial meetings to save money, did you see how many people ran to the mikes. They'd have nothing to do with that motion. 'We need each other. We have to meet like this every year,' they insisted.

"When the vote was called," Sally said, "I counted no more than ten hands raised in favor."

"During the communion service," Bill added, "I think I finally understood what 'the communion of saints' means."

"I hope this camaraderie prevails tomorrow when we get into the nitty-gritty," Joe said.

"Like homosexuality?"

"Yes." Joe pulled over to the curb to let Sally and Bill out. "I'll pick you up here about eight tomorrow. Okay?"

After they got off, Joe fell into introspection, grateful for how the three of them had hit it off and been inspired by the gathering. Yet, beneath the good feeling, he felt apprehensive. *We're great in the singing and hugging, but God, how will we fare when social issues come up?*

When he entered the house, Anita was watching TV. Since it was only 9:30, he knew he shouldn't ruin the program with church talk. He went to the kitchen and poured himself a glass of skim milk and made his usual cheese sandwich, then went back to the living room and sat on the sofa next to his wife.

"How'd it go?"

"Fine. Very inspirational. We won't get into real business till tomorrow. Hope it goes well but …." He stopped because the commercials were over, but he didn't bother to elaborate during the next advertising break.

Joe couldn't understand his own feelings. In spite of receiving inspiration, it didn't calm his unrest. When they headed for the bedroom, he said, "I doubt if I'll be able to sleep. Too much on my mind. In my younger days I could stand up under stress. It's much harder now. I really could use some golf."

Never did Joe take a sleeping pill before going to bed, but this night he broke his own rule and downed two PM tablets. During the few minutes before falling asleep, he felt so tired that he began thinking about his own death. He recalled the words from the prayer book: "May we go to our death as though we were going to the communion table." Thoughts of his father and others who had died rushed through his mind. He felt on the verge of some profound thought, when his body jerked and he fell sleep. He slept soundly until the chirping of birds aroused him. It was only five o'clock. *It must be the mating season for mocking birds. Or, do birds always wake this early? Do birds praise God with their songs?*

Then he remembered that it had been birds who had interrupted his dream about hiking at the *Togakushi* cliffs near Lake Nojiri. Like their neighbor, Harry Altman, who had fallen to his death from the cliff, Joe dreamt he was balancing his steps to pass over that same slippery path that bridged the ravine.

When Joe looked down on the left, he saw his cousin Teddy, who had been killed in a bleacher crash at Purdue. Going a little farther he peered down at a dead body stretched out on the limbs of a tree. Drawing closer, he recognized Teddy's brother, Arthur, who also had died. Frightened by such gruesome sights, Joe's legs began to shake. The path was too narrow to go back. The only way he could save himself was to pass over to the far side.

Pausing to clear his mind and quiet his wobbly legs, he gazed ahead. Standing in front of him stood a man with outstretched arms beckoning Joe to come to him.

When Joe finally reached the other side, he looked up into the face of the man who had been welcoming him. It was Joe's father. At that moment the songs of birds awakened him.

The clock read 5:00, but Joe knew he wouldn't be able to get back to sleep. He first must unravel the meaning of the dream. Not bothering to boil water for tea, he went straight to his recliner, but quickly changed his mind and walked over to the windows and drew open the drapes. Outside, the day was breaking. He picked up the flag by the front door and carried it outside and hoisted it into its slot, then went back to his chair.

What a surprise he saw! He looked out at the flag, but in the window's reflection he saw the large woodblock print by Sadao Watanabe hanging on the wall above the piano. The name of the work was "Sacrifice." To Joe, the kneeling figure looked like Jesus in the Garden of Gethsemane, framed by palm branches.

What does all this mean? Am I called to cross over some narrow precipice, not falling to my death on either side. Is Dad telling me all will be well, just keep going forward.

Joe realized then that the mocking birds were not mocking him, but praising God for the dawn of a new day.

27
Weeping

Joe put the kettle on the stove. He opened the refrigerator and pulled out his morning helping of almonds and vitamins. Pouring water onto a tea bag, he waited a few seconds to let the tea steep.

For a moment he was tempted to give the process some special meaning but gave up and took the pot and mug to the living room. While waiting for the hot tea to cool, he pulled out his Bible and prayer book. In the light of his dream, he anticipated that the lesson for the day would have some special guidance for him. Turning to Matthew 23:37, he read of Jesus' lament over Jerusalem. Joe then asked himself if he should weep like Jesus over what he saw.

The implications of that thought would take time to unravel; so he picked up his mug and coddled it between his hands. Outside, the dawn had dispersed the darkness, making the reflection of "Sacrifice" no longer visible. He had to imagine it. *What kind of sacrifice have I been called to make? I can't stay on the mountain side shedding sentimental tears.* He knew that a shallow response to the hurts of the church and world would be inadequate, for God searches man to the depth of his being. There are no shadows within his heart where he could hide. "Whither shall I go from thy spirit? Or whither shall I flee from thy presence? If I ascend up into heaven, thou art there: if I make my bed in hell, behold thou art there….If I say, Surely the darkness shall cover me; even the night shall be light about me."

Joe thumbed ahead in the prayer book to see which petition in the Lord's Prayer was to be meditated on. It turned out to be "Forgive us our trespasses as we forgive those who trespass against us." In the margin he read his shorthand for this: "Self-awareness." *Or, should I pray like some other churches do and say "forgive us our debts?" Which is better?*

How did he trespass on others? How did his judgments impinge on their personhood? Was he knowingly trespassing on the integrity of gays and lesbians? It hurt him to think of that. Had the expression on his face or the tone of his voice implied disapproval?

If he used *debt*, how could he be indebted to them, or they to him? What would that mean?

He sipped the tea which had become lukewarm and wondered if he might be a lukewarm believer whom God would spew out of his mouth.

Such thoughts were too hard to handle. Then he imagined that the weeping Jesus turned to look at him. "My peace I give you," Jesus said. "Let me handle your dilemma. It's okay to feel guilty and forgiven at the same time. You are not supposed to be God. Only I can hold onto contradictions and dissolve them in one great reach of outstretched painful love.

"I sent that dream to you in the night. You will not plunge to destruction on either the right or the left. Simply go forward. As your father welcomed you in the dream, so shall I. Be not afraid. I walk with you."

From that point on Joe believed all would be well, but how it would come about he hadn't a clue. He would just go forward in uncertain certainty. Without looking, he reached for his tea, knocking the mug over. Fortunately, the tea didn't spill onto the rug.

The morning spell of meditation had ended. It was time for a shower and breakfast before leaving for the Synod meeting.

"Did you see the note for you on the counter?" Anita greeted him when she returned from her morning swim. "The travel agent wants us to pay before she can mail us our plane tickets to Japan."

"I've already told her to put it on our American Express account. Could you call her this morning? Number is in the travel file."

"What time will you be home?"

"Not till late. It'll be a long day." He kissed her on the way out, but so quickly she complained.

"That was pathetic." So, he went back and did it right.

When Joe and his two youthful companions entered the hotel lobby, they could hear the organ signaling the delegates to hurry and take their seats.

The bishop introduced the preacher for the service, Hans Luger, who had been a student in the first class at the underground seminary which Dietrich Bonhoeffer had organized. As an opponent of Adolph Hitler's Nazi rule, Bonhoeffer eventually was martyred. Luger's thick German accent, stately manner and silvery hair thrown back in waves added to his impressiveness. He had been in Southern California for two decades, so he knew what issues would provoke the most debate. When he became specific, he mentioned the conflict over homosexuality and GLEE's efforts to influence the Synod. Then he abruptly lowered his voice, forcing everyone in the audience to stop all conversation and strain to hear his words.

Bill Scully pulled out his pen to write down what Luger had to say. He quoted from the patron saint of post-War Christendom, Dietrich Bonhoeffer. "'He who can no longer listen to his brother will soon be no longer listening to God either, he will be doing nothing but prattle in the presence of God.' Let me repeat that, repeat it slowly so that no one can say he or she did not hear it." Then he boomed out the same words, adding at the end more words from Bonhoeffer: 'We should listen with the ears of God that we may speak the Word of God.'" The auditorium became dead silent.

"My dear brothers and sisters in Christ, we are called to obedience. Each of us must examine his or her heart to discern what Jesus calls us to do at this time and place. The rest of the nation looks to California to set the trends of American society. As Jesus' disciples we must not shirk our responsibility."

"Wow!" Bill exclaimed. "Let me get this down." As though Luger had heard Bill, he repeated the admonition slowly so that no one could forget it.

Pausing with head down over the podium, he roared, "Amen and amen."

28
A Turning Point

The Assembly looked electrified by such a somber admonition. Joe realized that only someone who had lived through the dictatorial and pagan reign of Adolph Hitler could have spoken with such authority. The sermon seemed to alert the delegates that the Synod Assembly of 2004 could mark a turning point for the church.

"What does this mean?" Sally asked. "Are we witnessing some defining event for the church?"

"I didn't expect anything like this," Bill responded. "If Luger is right and California sets the agenda for the nation, this Assembly could determine the tone for the whole North American church."

"Good God, I feel tired already," Joe groaned, "and it's only 9:30. Let's go out for coffee and think about what's happening." They set their agenda packets on the table and headed toward the lobby. Down the aisle on the right he saw Wilbur Chan leading Isaiah Menkir and Sungdo Kim out of the hall. Joe wondered how they had received the sermon. They hardly could have imagined yesterday how important their voices might become today.

Weaving their way toward refreshments, Joe heard someone calling from behind. He turned around and saw Shinichi Katsunaga waving. "Wait for me," he called. To draw more attention he shouted it in Japanese, "*Matte kudasai.*"

Joining the three, Shinichi said, "Is there some place where we can talk?" He looked agitated.

"How about over behind the counter? No one is using those chairs." So, they circled to the back and pulled four chairs around a small table.

"Something bothering you?" Joe asked.

"I'm not sure what Pastor Luger was trying to tell us. What does he mean by 'California lifestyle'? I think I know, but he wasn't talking only about what people wear."

"You're right." Joe stared at Shinichi. "You're like me. You're wearing a dark suit. My wife would never let me go to a Synod Assembly in shirt sleeves."

"I'm also like that."

Bill and Sally were listening with keen interest. "I assumed delegates would be wearing sport shirts," Bill said. "I did see one pastor in full black-crow suit and clerical collar."

"More than clothing, it's attitude, isn't it?" Sally asked. "Many people who moved here from the East came to get away from old traditions, including the church."

"Don't forget the influx from Asia," Joe said. "We've got every religion imaginable, Hinduism, Buddhism in all varieties and a twenty-first-century version of gnosticism wrongly called New Age. It's quite a mix.

"Recently a sociology professor lectured at the seminary. He said California has gone secular. The only stories that attract are the ones in the movies and TV. They're mostly of evil made glamorous. These secular waves sweep across the country, gradually eroding the moral fabric of the nation."

The sound of singing filtered into the lobby, signaling that the first business session was about to begin.

"Shinichi, we're a minority movement. That's why, I think, Luger drew on the German experience under Hitler. It's time for us in America to draw a line in the sand, make a stand. We've retreated too far already. He claims it's time for radical obedience."

"You Japanese Christians went through a lot in the War," Sally said. "I've read about how hard it was for your people to stand firm when the police made you declare who was supreme, Jesus or the Emperor."

"We'd better go back to our seats," Joe said. "Let's see if we can eat lunch with Wilbur Chan, Menkir and Kim. Okay? Let's meet here after we've picked up our box lunches."

The rest of the morning was taken up with the Bishop's State of the Synod Address, the financial report and greetings from the heads of synodical institutions. By the written agenda, it looked as though GLEE had managed to get a choice time on the agenda: 2:00 p.m. Matters pertaining to the so-called minority ethnic churches and Hispanics would come later.

"Bill, do you think you could find Chan and the other two? Ask if we can meet over lunch. We'll need to get our act together to react to GLEE's recommendations. They're going to come on strong. We need to figure out how we should respond. We don't want to give a divided opinion."

"Aren't you playing politics?" Sally warned.

"If we are, isn't it necessary? To think through different scenarios is only common sense." She shook her head, as though disillusioned by this kind of talk. Katsunaga looked perplexed. "I wonder what position our Japanese church would take?"

Joe saw that Bill had found Chan and his group. By the looks on their faces and Bill's pointing toward the lobby refreshment stand, they had agreed to meet over lunch.

"We're all set then. Let's get the drift of the Assembly so that this afternoon we can go with the flow. Or, swim against it."

29
Strategy

"I wish we had my daughter's sheltie sheepdog here," Joe said as they waited behind the counter. "He'd round up our fellows in no time."

Chan, Kim and Menkir eventually arrived, carrying their box lunches and cold drinks.

"Sorry to ask you to meet, but it seemed a good idea to figure out how we should react to the resolution from the gay/lesbian caucus."

"Do we need to answer?" Chan asked.

"I don't see why," said Kim. "We shouldn't push our views too much."

"I'm thinking the same way," Katsunaga added. "If we just stick to our own resolution, that's enough."

"Isn't it true that any decisions at the Synod level don't automatically go into effect?" Bill asked. "They're only recommendations to the national Assembly. Am I right on that?"

"So, why try to oppose GLEE's motion?" Menkir asked.

"But if it's true that California sets the nation's agenda, shouldn't we take this seriously?" countered Joe.

"Forgive me for speaking, but can't we take a middle path?" Katsunaga asked. "I don't pretend to understand all this, but it seems to me we could back GLEE. While we voice support, one of us could raise some issues that may have been overlooked."

"For instance? What do you have in mind?" Bill asked.

"Since coming to America, I took time to read the Constitution of the Concordia Lutheran Church. As I read it, I realized we might be breaking the Constitution by going along with GLEE. I brought it along. Let me read it. It says that congregations 'accept the canonical Scriptures of the Old and New Testaments as the inspired Word of God and the authoritative source and norm of its proclamation, faith and life.'"

"Really?" Joe said.

"What's the point?" Menkir asked.

"I get it," said Chan. "If GLEE's proposals sanction homosexual practices, they would be obligated to prove they're in compliance with Scripture."

"Shinichi, you may have hit on a fundamental issue," Joe said.

"If our church follows GLEE's reasoning," Bill said, "then we first must amend the Constitution. But if we state our concern too bluntly, wouldn't there be a backlash?"

"We are full voting members in America, but to many in the church, we're still foreigners. Maybe we should soften our opinion."

"How?" Menkir asked.

"Well, what we would probably do in Japan is not oppose the GLEE motion head on. Support the motion, but then request that the proper committee of the national church study its constitutionality."

"Is there a standing committee that handles stuff like that?" Bill asked.

"There is, but I don't know what it's called,"said Joe. "It's something like the Doctrinal Adjudication Committee or Theological Commission. It's like a Rules of Order Committee to deal with gray areas."

"If we do that, we won't sound too contentious," Chan said. "I like that approach."

"There's another potential problem," Joe said. "That's the legality of whatever the church decides. In these days of sexual scandals, we can't be too careful. Even if what we do is legal and right, it must appear to be so. We had an oil corporation's PR man in Tokyo talk to us media people. He made a big point of saying, 'We must not just be good, but appear (to outsiders) to be good.' Nowadays we don't dare hug parishioners or children. Teachers are in the same boat."

Wilbur Chan then tried to state the group's mutual understanding. "We agree, don't we, that someone should ask about the Constitution? Okay? Who should raise that question?"

They all looked at each other, but in the end their eyes focused on Katsunaga. Sungdo Kim spoke. "He's the only one of us who has read the Constitution — at least lately."

"I would be too nervous," Shinichi said.

"No problem," Bill quickly responded. "We can write it down. Then read it, as a motion."

"Menkir, why don't you second it?" Joe suggested.

"What about legal issues?" Chan asked.

"You Chinese in Hong Kong have been struggling over such matters a lot these days. You ought to do it," Menkir said, "maybe suggest the Church's attorney handle it."

"All of us should be free to speak," Chan said. "That will strengthen our position. Do we need to discuss anything else? If not, could you gather in a little closer. Pastor Kim, you Koreans are famous for your prayer meetings. Would you close our time with prayer?"

It caught Kim by surprise, but he quickly threw his spirit into a prayerful mode and began to speak to God as if God were present with them. He might have prayed on and on, but the sound of the loud speaker drowned him out; so he slowed to a stop and ended by saying, "and may all our needs and those of our families be met, for Jesus' sake. Amen."

30
Synodical Skirmish

A fanfare blared from the organ, summoning delegates to the afternoon session. Bishop Friberg stood up. "The Agenda Committee has an urgent request. Will you state your motion."

The Committee chairperson spoke from the standing microphone in the center aisle. "Twenty-five delegates have presented a signed petition for immediate action. It reads, 'Because of the unprecedented and questionable actions taken by the city of San Francisco to issue marriage licenses to same-sex couples, clergy of our church should not conduct Christian wedding ceremonies for any of them. If in the future, the California courts rule that same-sex marriages are legal, this church should reconsider its ban.'"

Since the provision for reconsideration was included in the petition, it passed immediately by voice vote.

Bishop Friberg then asked the Gays and Lesbians for Evangelical Equality to present its resolution. Dr. Michael McGibbon strode briskly to the microphone. "We of the Gays and Lesbians for Evangelical Equality propose that (1) the restrictions on blessing same-sex unions be rescinded, and that (2) the prohibition on ordaining non-celibate homosexuals be abolished."

Buzzing among delegates became so loud that the Bishop pounded his gavel on the lecturn. "Will the meeting come to order. Order," he shouted. "Order, please come to order."

Joe motioned for Wilbur Chan to go to the microphone. Picking up his notes Chan ran up the right aisle. Grabbing the microphone, he lowered it to mouth level, then spoke. "Mr. Moderator, Mr. Moderator." Still not heard, he shouted, "Bishop Friberg."

"State your name please."

"I am Pastor Wilbur Chan. I am speaking on behalf of the foreign-language ethnic churches of our Synod. In anticipation of the resolution from GLEE, we wish to express our thanks to them for their forthright proposal. In our discussions in the ethnic caucus, one of our newest pastors, the Reverend Shinichi Katsunaga, raised a question we had not heard before. I think he should explain it to the Assembly."

Katsunaga, who had taken his place next to Chan, moved to the mike. "After coming to the Yorba Linda Japanese church, I thought I should read the Constitution of Concordia Church. It's very similar to ours in Japan. On the question of authority, it reads, 'the congregations accept the canonical Scriptures of the Old and New Testaments as the inspired Word of God and the authoritative source and norm of its proclamation, faith and life.'

"What troubles me about the arguments over same-sex matters is that we could go against the church's Constitution."

All buzzing among the delegates halted.

Chan again took over the mike. "While we see merit in GLEE's position, we think its legality must first be clarified. Should we not request the national church's appropriate committee to study this before acting? Also we feel that the implications regarding the law and how we will be viewed by others should be examined. Pastor Katsunaga told us that we must not only be good, but be seen by outsiders to be good.

"Since California often begins national trends, we must be cautious in making changes of policy. We might start something that cannot be stopped. Also what the American church does must not prove damaging to sister churches in other parts of the world. We are a world church. We Americans must not act unilaterally."

There was a stunned silence in the auditorium.

"Thank you for sharing this with us," Bishop Friberg said. It took a few minutes for the impact of Chan and Katsunaga's comments to sink in. Before anyone else could speak, Isaiah Menkir reached the mike in the center aisle. "Mr. Moderator, I second the views expressed by Pastors Chan and Katsunaga. Let's pass both GLEE's motion and the one calling for study."

A voice shouted from the back. "Question! I call for the vote."

Bishop Friberg looked flustered, not knowing how to proceed. He took a deep breath, then seemed relieved that the sexuality issues could be disposed with so quickly. "All in favor, say 'Aye.'" Pausing a moment, he asked "Against? The motion passes unanimously."

The reporters in the press section headed for the lobby. They had heard what they came for. That would be the heart of their stories for the morning papers and evening newscasts.

"Whew," Joe sighed. "That was something. Let's go outside for a drink. Something cold would taste good. He, Bill and Sally left the hall and headed for the barrels where cold drinks were kept on ice. Dr. McGibbon soon arrived at their side. "You guys think you're smart, don't you?" he said. "I have to hand it to you. But this fight is far from over."

31
Uneasiness

That night as Joe tried to fall asleep, McGibbon's warning troubled him. GLEE had backers in the national gay and lesbian movement. They would not sit back and let this minor detour go unchallenged. Joe's premonition proved right. In the morning, when he opened the *Chronicle,* the front page of the California section carried the headline: "Gays Denounce Lutheran Decision." In the meat of the article the gay spokesman attacked the Synod for listening to the foreign-born clergy. "They don't know how hard the decision will be for church members waiting to have their sexual partnerships consecrated by the church.

"Dr. Michael McGibbon of the Theological Seminary of the West decried the delay in ordaining qualified clergy candidates. 'This is a civil rights issue,' he declared. 'If the church baptizes gay and lesbian people, they should not be excluded from professional leadership positions.'

"When Ethiopian pastor Isaiah Menkir was asked about it, he said that the members in the foreign-language ethnic churches hold a high view of the Bible. For conscience sake they will not defy the Bible's clear injunctions against homosexual activity. In such countries as Ethiopia, Indonesia and Malaysia our Christians are surrounded by Muslims for whom sodomy is a gross violation of God's commands. If Christians sanction same-sex activities, they will be regarded as degenerate. No one will give an ear to persons whom they consider corrupt."

When Joe finished reading the article, he shook his head. *How can we ever resolve all this?*

At eight o'clock, he picked up Sally and Bill. As soon as they were in the car, Bill said, "Have you seen the Inland Valley Gazette? There's a photo of Chan and Katsunaga shaking hands with McGibbon. The caption says, 'Opponents, Yet Friends.' Underneath it tells of GLEE's proposal and the one from the ethnic pastors. It's a rather fair account of both positions. At the end, it quotes McGibbon saying, 'The church must not be bound by a narrow fundamentalistic interpretation of the Bible. The twenty-first century is different from biblical times. Even words have changed their meanings. But the bottom line is: What would Jesus do? I can't imagine him discriminating against someone on the basis of sexual orientation.'"

Sally spoke up. "I was surprised at how quickly the vote was taken. It looked as though Bishop Friberg purposely rushed it."

"In Japan," Joe said, "we had a church president whom we suspected of purposely delaying votes on important issues until just before adjournment time. Delegates would be thinning out the hall and hurrying to catch trains so no one wanted to stay and debate."

As Joe parked the car at the hotel, he heard someone calling him. It was Carl Johnson and his wife Marty from Temecula. "Joe, did you have something to do with that Japanese pastor's idea?"

"I know him, but the point about the church Constitution was his own."

"He caught the GLEE people off balance, but McGibbon and his friends will keep pushing on this."

"That's for sure," Joe agreed. "We know each other pretty well. He's been hurt badly about his sexuality."

"Wasn't he married before? I heard he deserted his wife. They had two kids. When he came out, the marriage collapsed," Carl said. "That often happens. She's Danish — a happy Dane, not a legalistic holy one. But holy enough to lay down the law. I'm told she once called him 'a dirty old man.'"

"That's not true," Joe said. They separated amiably I've been told. Tough on the kids though."

"Someone said she left Berkeley and moved down here to LaVerne."

"Were you here yesterday? I didn't see you."

"I had to see my doctor; so I came at noon. We want to do a segment on the same-sex marriage issue for television. Would you introduce me to that Rev. Chan and what's his name, Katsuwagi?"

"Katsunaga. You should also meet the Ethiopian, Isaiah Menkir."

"Would you broadcast it?"

"Actually, I've been thinking more of a video to sell. This topic is hot, and lots of Lutherans would want to hear these ideas from people who grew up overseas."

"You should use McGibbon, too," Joe suggested. "He comes to the issue with a great deal of feeling. I'd stay away from his ex-wife Elna. She could fall apart on camera."

"Could you contact them and try to get them to meet me during the lunch break?"

"I can try. Where should we meet? How about the registration desk? Right after the morning session. Okay?"

32
Return to Hiroshima

Joe was on a high. He hadn't functioned at a church convention for years. Although the stateside procedures differed from Japan, he was surprised how smoothly he adjusted.

He had worked behind the scenes with the ethnic pastors, a little like a *kurokko*, a puppeteer. He didn't think that he had manipulated them but only helped let things happen naturally. It was as though he had been praying about matters and stepped aside to let God work His way. Everything seemed oiled to mesh perfectly with other moving parts.

Joe felt fortunate he could still play a role in American church life. When he first retired from Japan, he told people that it would take him five years to get used to America. It had been almost exactly five years when his wife told him after he had stood talking on the phone: "Joe, do you realize you're no longer bowing to people when you talk to them?"

"Really? When we leave for Japan next week, do you think I'll fall back into my old ways?"

In the past, it had not taken him long to regain his fluency in Japanese. Sometimes he couldn't come up with the right word, but usually his sub-conscious mind took over so that even the most difficult words eventually would come out.

With each passing time zone on the way from Los Angeles, he became more excited. At Narita airport they activated Japan Rail passes and were soon speeding through the countryside and suburbs to Tokyo. While they waited to change to a commuter train, Anita called their son's home, but no one answered. Since they hadn't much luggage, they decided to walk the ten minutes from the final station and surprise the family. After some drinks and conversation, they all went to bed.

The next morning, they took off for their original place of work, Hiroshima City. Instead of a long tiring overnight trip of fifteen hours as in 1950, this time they rode a bullet train that took only six hours. The transition from California, to Tokyo, to Hiroshima happened too fast for them. They hardly had time to realize that they were moving back to a time in their life fifty-four years ago. In front of the station, classy Toyota sedans waited for customers, not the old three-wheelers and green Renaults of 1950. There were no more open-air noodle shops on the street, only orderly lines for modern buses fueled by gasoline, not charcoal. The street cars and tracks were gone.

Getting in a shiny black taxi, Joe said, *"Tsurumi-cho, Ruteru Kyokai"* (The Lutheran Church at Tsurumi). The car sped along wide avenues, eventually taking a shortcut down a narrow road.

"I used to walk this way from the station," Joe told the driver. They saw no flimsy post-war houses, only elegant ones, interspersed with tall apartment buildings. "The church is ten floors high." As they came to the 100-meter-wide Peace Boulevard, Anita pointed ahead at the new magnificent church. The taxi pulled up in front just as a bride and groom were boarding a black limousine.

It was quite a contrast to what Pastor Kiyoshi Watanabe and Joe found on this lot in 1951. Then there was only a small frame house that doubled for parsonage and church. Their vision was being fulfilled by this new structure.

Several church members came to greet the Weavers. "We'll take your bags to the guest room. Go over by the stairs. That's the pastor seeing off the wedding couple."

Afterward he came over to welcome Anita and Joe. "It's best to approach the church by these stairs," he said.

They looked up. On the front of the building hung a twenty-foot metal cross. Halfway up the three flights of stairs, to the left a stick-like bronze figure of the Good Shepherd with a lamb across his shoulder looked down on them. As they puffed their way up to the top of the stairs, they stopped to contemplate the Savior watching over them.

Reaching the top of the stairs, straight ahead they saw on the wall, engraved in Japanese and Greek:

"My house shall be a house of prayer for all nations."

To the left was a huge poster which read, "World Peace Conference, August 6-9, 2005, 60th anniversary of the atomic bombing."

They turned to enter the foyer. As they passed through the open door, they heard a recorded voice saying, "Welcome to our sanctuary. Feel free to enter and pray."

Staring into the huge worship space, they saw bright red Pentecost paraments and candles above the altar, representing the descent of the Holy Spirit. Anita and Joe stood in awe. Also above the altar was a stick-like bronze figure of the crucified Jesus stretching out his arms as if to embrace all people.

"What a wonderful place to hold a peace conference!" Joe exclaimed. He looked at his wife and knew she felt as he did. They wondered if they shouldn't return to Hiroshima the following August.

33
Called to Speak

As soon as they returned to Tokyo, Anita went to their son's computer to access E-mail messages. She quickly returned to the living room.

"Joe, look at this. It's from Dr. Henke of the mission board. He wants you to speak at the General Assembly."

"Good heavens! You must be kidding."

"I kid you not. They heard from Isaiah Menkir how much you had meant to the ethnic pastors. They think you're the one who could bridge the chasm that's developed between the American and overseas churches.

"Here, I printed it out." She handed it to Joe. "He mentions your book about *Pre-emptive Love*, and he even says nice words about *'Iesu*, let it be' from your golfing book."

"God certainly works in mysterious ways. I wonder if someone ever tipped them off about my college oration on "Those Spaces." It was all about the spaces in society that needed to be bridged. Isn't it amazing how the theme of reconciliation has run through my life? No wonder people speak of God as 'the Great Scriptwriter.'"

"He wants you to send them your sermon topic and text by the end of June."

"Tell him 'Yes' by the grace of God. I'm almost eighty years old." He paused. "How old was Abraham when he left Haran?"

"Seventy-five."

Son Jim, who had been listening, finally spoke. "You can do it. Your whole life has been a preparation for a chance like this."

"If I didn't have Anita and a great family — and the promise of God's help, I could never think of saying 'Yes' to this invitation. If it's a call from God, then He'll help me do it."

As soon as he said this, the faces of Chan, Katsunaga, Kim and Menkir flashed before his eyes, then the faces of Sally and Bill, followed by McGibbon. "In speaking," he continued, "we were taught to focus on one person. At least that was true for radio. Keep the face of that person in mind. It's the sure way to prevent pompous hot air. Just talk to an individual or small group."

Following their two weeks in Japan, they looked forward to returning to America. After their flight, they used the shuttle service from Los Angeles and arrived at their house too late for the noon meal at Eternally Young. Instead, Joe opened a can of vegetable soup and made a sandwich with hardtack. Anita settled for a poached egg and frozen waffle.

She went to the study to check E-mails. By the time she had finished, her waffle was cold and the egg boiled hard. To her, E-mails pre-empted food.

Joe turned the TV on to CNN for Headline News.

"Joe, come here. You've got to see this letter from Dr. Henke. There's trouble over your speaking."

"What? Who is stirring up a fuss?"

"You read it. Look at the bottom paragraph."

He scanned the first two paragraphs, then the last one, which said: "I have to tell you that not everyone is pleased that our Division for Overseas Mission selected you to be the speaker for the 'World Mission Emphasis.' As best as I can determine, several persons on the Sexuality Task Force object to you because they heard you were involved with the petitions from Southern California. Is there any truth to their concerns? Please reply ASAP. Gerald Henke.

"Sounds like McGibbon's work or some others from GLEE."

"Why don't you call Dr. Henke? He'll still be in the office. It's only 3:00 their time. You've got to clear this up."

"I'll use the cell phone. That's free. He punched in the numbers and waited. In a few seconds, Henke was on the line. After friendly greetings, Joe asked about the objections.

"Somehow," Henke began, "they — that is several men on the task force think you are interfering with their study process. One member supposedly said, 'Foreigners should not interfere with us.'"

"They're not foreigners. Most of them are legitimate clergy in the CLC."

"I know that, but some of these people have already concluded what the outcome of their investigation should be. They thought they had covered all the bases. Then came the surprising news from Southern California. They've wanted to choreograph the church's Assembly proceedings, so that everything works out according to their script."

"Sounds familiar. No wonder the grassroots get upset. They feel they're left out of the process."

"Does the name *McGibbon* mean anything to you?"

"Certainly does. Is he in cahoots with them?"

"I think so."

"He's basically a good man, gay himself. His homosexuality destroyed his marriage. Had a wife and two kids. He's been hurt badly. He's the leading guru for GLEE out here."

"I see."

"I'll try to see him before the Assembly. I don't believe in hurting him more. He's an honest advocate for gay rights, but he's willing to listen. We shouldn't treat people as our enemies."

"I'm glad to hear you say that. You must be tired. We can talk again in a few days."

Joe set the phone down. "Henke's a good man, very open and fair. Our mission board people have all been that way, even that treasurer who put the screws on our expansion plans. The church has been good to us. Now it's payback time. I hope I can meet their expectations."

35
Unexpected Request

"Can you meet Dr. Henke's expectations?" Anita asked.

Joe hesitated, shocked at his wife's doubts. "It's a tall order. One thing I know is that I must spread hope to the church."

"Hope? How do you mean?"

"Our country is torn apart these days because of the presidential election. People hunger for good news."

"What if the Iraq war gets worse by August?" she asked.

"All the more reason to preach hope."

"But you don't have wordsmiths to spin your speech like Bush and Kerry."

"When I speak, I won't be tooting my own horn. I'll be witnessing. If I can tell truth as it is, it will be believable. D.T. Niles of Sri Lanka once said, 'I must be like a beggar telling other beggars where to find food.' If I'm truthful about myself, not putting on airs, people will listen."

"Henke asked you to speak largely because you worked well with the ethnic pastors. Why not expand on that? Ask for their help."

"What do you have in mind?"

"They must have some insights and know stories that can re-enforce whatever you say. You might even get some visuals to put up on the screen, but you'd have to do it well."

"I don't know. You really think I should ask them? I'd better sleep on it."

Joe did try to sleep on it that night. While lying in bed, he tried to compose a letter to the pastors. To bring about reconciliation over the sexuality issues, wouldn't he have to begin by confessing his own guilt? He had trespassed against his brothers and sisters. The more he thought about it, the more regretful events in his past came to mind: poking fun at Jimmy Durham for his effeminate ways, teasing bashful guys in the shower room, joking about manly women. On and on he recalled his prejudices. Then Jacob the Old Testament rascal who cheated Esau out of both his inheritance and his father's blessing came to mind. But God intervened. He made a covenant with Jacob as he slept with a rock as a pillow, showing him angels descending and ascending on a ladder that reached to heaven.

Could I be repeating Jacob's experience? My pillow is not a rock but one stuffed with feathers. Could God be promising me a hopeful future, reconciling me with the people whom I have deceived and cheated?

Joe did not wrestle with God's messenger in the night. But every time he was on the verge of sleep, a new cause for guilt or a fresh insight aroused him. Not until he had given up and downed two PM tablets did he fall asleep.

In the morning, he awoke ten minutes before the alarm was to go off. In spite of the sleeping aids, he felt alert and ready to write to the pastors. He went to the study and picked up an unused pad of lined paper, then set it next to his recliner. Instead of boiling water for tea, he chose to heat leftover coffee and get on with his writing.

Returning to his chair, he began the letter to the ethnic pastors.

> Dear brothers and sisters in Christ,
> I cannot thank you enough for your contribution at the Synod meeting. News of what our Lord accomplished through you has reached the leaders of our church in Milwaukee.
> Dr. Gerald Henke, General Director of the CLC Division for Overseas Mission, wrote, asking me to

speak at the Church's General Assembly during the world mission rally.

I am sure that he asked me because he heard about the role you played at the Southern California Synod Assembly.

In discussing the request by phone with Dr. Henke, we agreed that the emphasis of my address should be on reconciliation. He recognized that we were not putting down gays and lesbians; so he thinks we might become the reconciling bridge to hold our church together.

Therefore, may I enlist your inspiration and wisdom? Concretely, can you suggest ideas and share examples that I could use in the presentation. Audio-visual capability will be available to enhance the message.

Would you help me perform this call for the sake of Christ and the church. Please respond by E-mail, phone or fax. I thank you for your partnership in this mission.

Cordially in Christ, Joseph Weaver

When Anita came back from her morning swim, Joe read the draft of the letter to her.

"Good. You've said it well." She started toward the bedroom but stopped to add, "What about stating a deadline for responses?"

"Good idea. I'll simply say, 'Reply no later than June 30th.'"

36
Second Thoughts

Why Dr. Henke asked Joe to be the speaker at the mission rally still perplexed him. The invitation had come unexpectedly and very late. It was not until the church's monthly magazine arrived that he found out. The news section carried a notice of the death of Dr. Ambrose Kim. In the last sentence, it said, "Kim had been scheduled to address the CLC General Assembly, but he died in a car crash near Seoul, Korea."

That news deflated Joe. He had not been Dr. Henke's first choice. Strange, he thought. how much hubris can infect us humans. Then on second thought, he recalled how often second choices become the best ones. If Joe really believed what he taught, he would commit the whole process to God: Let go and let God. Really be a spiritual beggar, only pointing other beggars to where food can be found.

Since reconciliation was to be the focus of the rally, he took that to mean personal as well as corporate. In Japan, he had always tried to be a reconciler. Often he advised people not to let roadblocks stymie them. Second choices of direction can become the best. In his marriage, he believed God had been guiding the circumstances that brought him and Anita together.

Since Joe would celebrate his 80th birthday in July, he had no qualms of conscience about reminiscing about his life. God had been good; He had preserved them from serious illness, assigned meaningful work, and blessed them with three children who served in healing occupations.

"Unto whom much has been given shall much be required" were words he took to heart. Joe had received abundantly. How could he ever repay God? He was permanently indebted to Him; yet God never laid on him a load of guilt. He did the opposite, carrying the weight himself so that Joe could move freely, 'sitting lightly in his saddle of life.'"

The more he thought of God's blessings, the more he felt obligated to share that same lightness of spirit with the delegates at the mission rally. He realized they would be wound up tight over the U.S. presidential campaign which could divide friends from friends, even alienating members in the same family. Joe, at one time, had even thought of putting up signs in his yard for Kerry, Bush and Nader to show his open spirit.

With the passage of the constitutional amendment in Missouri limiting marriage to a man and a woman, and the judge's ruling in Washington state to allow same-sex marriages, that debate would become more intense at the Assembly. Whenever married heterosexual couples bragged about how same-sex marriages are not an issue, Joe could only say how naive they were. Persons who treat marriage as a sacrament or holy institution will never let their clergy dilute the sacredness of marriage.

How can an 80-year-old outsider like me say the word that can heal division and strengthen the bonds of unity? He looked at the ceiling and whispered under his breath, "O God, you've got to help me."

Joe then reflected on how he could show a genuine humility that would not look phoney. Maybe that's the way to begin, confessing how hard it is to appear real. It has to be from within, not an acted performance. The audience should not think of him as another salesman. It should be as though people overheard Joe in the privacy of his home, like listening in on his innermost thoughts.

People might be turned off by his honesty. But he hoped the candid-camera shots of his own failures would touch people's secret wounds, lance their sores so that true healing could happen.

Suddenly Joe stopped his introspection. His thoughts had wandered too far from reconciliation. He must combine his musings with the challenge of building a testimonial speech that could heal the tender, black-and-blue bruises in people's souls.

"For goodness sake, Joe," his conscience said. "You've never worked in counseling, face to face with desperate souls. You've listened a few times. You tried but weren't you more a strategist for attracting outsiders to the church but weak at closing the deal at the personal level?"

"But, Lord, could that not have been advantageous for me? Not to know whom one has helped may be best. Only God really heals. We shouldn't expect to be given credit. Yet, at the mission rally at the General Assembly, Dr. Henke is recognizing me. Don't let me betray his trust in me."

37
Road Closed

August 6th was special for the Weavers. It marked the anniversary of the bombing of Hiroshima. They were pleased to arrive at the Eternally Young vesper service and read at the top of the bulletin that the event had not been forgotten.

"The Atomic Bomb exploded over Hiroshima, Japan just before this hour local time 59 years ago. Weapons of Mass Destruction continue to explode...."

The worship leader spoke passionately about Christians' responsibility to witness for peace. Joe admired his eloquence which moved the service along at a hectic pace but too fast for Joe to meditate on the words. He knew the speaker had chosen them carefully, so he folded the printed text of his sermon and put it into his pocket to study later. The call to reconciliation had hit home. He hoped the speaker's words would expand Joe's own horizons.

Later that anniversary day brought a surprise phone call. It was from a former resident in Hiroshima who wanted someone with whom to talk about Weapons of Mass Destruction. She complained that no papers or stations in Iowa bothered to mention Hiroshima that day. Immediate worries over Iraq and Al Queda monopolized the news.

Earlier that morning Joe played golf at the Claremont Course, afterward going to church for coffee with his buddies. They tried to hear each other over the noisy din coming from the Vacation Bible School kids. How wonderful he thought to be living in peace and safety as he watched the children's cheerful faces. It seemed near blasphemy for Joe to think any dark thoughts, but over coffee one of the golfers said, "Did you know that the crow population has decreased 60 percent? The West Nile virus is playing havoc with birds. I saw two dead ones yesterday."

"We've been told not to touch them," Joe said. "Get a shovel and put the dead bird in a plastic bag then throw it into the trash bin."

"What are the symptons for the virus?" the other golfer asked.

"Like flu. We've got so many trees in Claremont that lots of birds congregate here. Best not to leave water standing around for mosquitoes to breed."

The next morning when Joe arose, he felt more aches than usual. When he did his morning reading, he found himself sneezing a great deal.

"Must be a high pollen count today," he told his wife. By the time he had drunk his second cup of tea, he had used five sheets of tissue.

"I'm glad it's not a golf day. I feel lousy. Touch my forehead. Do I have a fever?"

She came and leaned over to feel him. "A little warm. You had better lie low today."

After sipping the rest of his tea, he pushed the LAY-Z-BOY back, closed his eyes and soon fell asleep. He awoke about 9:00 and went to the kitchen for breakfast. He poured a glass of orange juice for swallowing his vitamins."I'm skipping eggs and bacon. I'll try a big bowl of All Bran with sliced bananas." Rather than eat at the dining room table, he took a tray to his recliner.

"Anita, would you give the nurse a call? Someone should be on duty by now."

He heard her speaking to Lisa, the second in command. "I've a sick husband here. It looks like he's coming down with the flu." She waited for the nurse to respond, then said, "You don't know of any people here with the flu? Maybe you should look at him when you have time."

Joe finished breakfast, set the tray on the floor and leaned back for another snooze. No sooner had he drifted into sleep when the doorbell rang.

"Dang it! I was just about asleep."

Anita went to the door. "That was fast. Come in Lisa. He's over there in the corner."

"You don't look sick," the nurse said.

"You look pretty good yourself," he quipped back. Lisa knew Joe pretty well and had borne the brunt of his humor before.

"Let's see if you have a fever." She stuck a thermometer in his mouth. "Has he been like this long?"

"No, it hit him this morning."

"Umm," she murmured. "That's awfully sudden." She reached for the thermometer and held it up to the light. "He has something alright, 100 degrees. This could go higher by afternoon."

"I didn't think he was that hot," Anita said.

"Who is your doctor?"

"Duma," Joe answered.

"I don't think we can wait till Monday. I'll call him."

The strained look on Lisa's face worried Joe. "Could it be serious?"

"Have you been back to Asia this summer?"

"Late May and June for two weeks."

"Which countries?"

"Only Japan."

Lisa looked relieved. "I doubt if it's SARS then. Have any mosquitoes bit you?"

"What? Why?"

"The West Nile virus is killing a lot of birds in the area. Haven't you noticed the crows are gone? I'm not a doctor. I'll call Dr. Duma. In the meantime drink plenty of liquids. Stay off the beer."

"How'd you know I like beer?"

"I've seen all the empty cans in front of your house."

"No secrets at Eternally Young," Anita blushed. "I told you not to leave them out there for everyone to see."

"We have to keep up appearances," Joe laughed in the direction of the nurse.

"You get your rest," she ordered.

"Great! This morning I was going to start on my sermon for a mission rally. Now it looks as though I may never give that address."

"You might not have the virus, but we need to make sure. I'll call you after I speak with the doctor."

38
Diagnosis

The phone rang about 11:00. Anita answered in the bedroom, but Joe could overhear the conversation because he put the cordless phone to his ear.

"This is Lisa. I talked with Dr. Duma and told him what I knew: aching muscles and joints, slight rash, headache and fever. He can't see Mr. Weaver today, but he has ordered a private room at the Pomona Valley Hospital. He's almost certain it's the West Nile virus. He'll know after some blood tests. The ER doctors know what to do."

"That doesn't sound too hopeful," Anita said.

"If you're strong enough, Mrs. Weaver can drive you there this afternoon. They have Duma's instructions. Just go and check in at the Emergency Room."

"Thanks, Lisa."

"Yes, thanks," Joe added.

Anita came in to the living room and sat on the sofa opposite Joe. "I hope they can get to the bottom of this and find out what's wrong with you."

He was tempted to snap back at her by repeating her words, "what's wrong with you?" but was too tired for joking. "You know I'm not very good at being sick. At least I have no pain, just a weak limpness. Would you hand me my black bag? I'll put my small Bible and prayer book in there along with those yellow tablets with writing on them. I'll put in a clean pad, too. They're by the printer. Under the newspaper you'll find the latest golf magazines and *The Writer*. I'll stick them in, too."

"I don't think you'll be up to reading. I'll bring the crucifix I put up for you last time."

Joe examined his datebook. "Ani, could you call Pastor Katsunaga and tell him what's happening? I hope he has some good examples for my mission talk. Also call Bill Scully. You can E-mail the ethnic pastors and ask for material as soon as possible.

"E-mail Dr. Henke. Tell him my sermon topic is 'Bridging the Chasm.' Bible texts are Galatians 2:19-21 and Acts 15:6-21. Don't tell him I'm sick."

After lunch and a brief nap, Anita and Joe headed for the hospital in Pomona. He much preferred being driven by his wife than by the 911 medics. Check-in went smoothly, then a masked volunteer pushed him in a wheelchair to his room. It was small, not like the big one he had shared when he had surgery eight years before. It was more a post-operative holding room, but it did have a TV up on the wall.

"Can you tell if it can get WGN? Cubs play the Giants tonight."

"You'd better forget TV and act a little sick."

Soon a masked orderlie arrived with standard hospital wear. "Behind that door you have a small toilet," he said. "Make yourself at home."

"What a choice of words!" Joe said to Anita afterward. "Hospitals can't be like home, no matter how nice and pretty the nurses are."

Anita drew up a chair. In a few minutes, the volunteer returned with the wheelchair. "Time for your blood tests," he announced.

"That was fast," Anita said.

"Ma'am, I'm afraid you'll have to leave. We need to keep your husband isolated."

"Oh, for goodness sake," and she grasped his arm. Looking into his eyes, she said, "We're not going to panic." She headed toward the door ahead of Joe. When the volunteer closed the door, he looked back at the sign stuck on the door which read, "No admittance" and had the same insignia as the "No-Entry" signs on one-way streets.

Anita waved goodbye and sadly retreated in the opposite direction. The sense of loneliness reminded him of the moonless night when he walked up an unfamiliar road to the Hoki home in Gota Village. But just like then, he knew God was walking with him.

He was wheeled into the testing room. One young male doctor and two nurses motioned him in. Each wore a surgical mask. Their eyes emitted kindness.

"This won't hurt," the doctor asssured him as he helped Joe onto a sheet-covered gurney.

"Lord, you have brought me this far. Let it all work for good," he prayed beneath his breath.

39
Not Abandoned

No one explained anything to Joe. He wondered what they were looking for. Within half an hour, he had been wheeled back to his room to face the long night with neither wife nor friends. All he had were his reading materials which he soon realized didn't interest him now. He'd have to hear the results of the blood test before he could think about preparing his talk.

A nurse brought him supper at 5:00, but he hardly touched it. He tried the TV, but it didn't carry WGN. That ruled out the Cubs' game. Instead he found a PBS channel that was broadcasting 'Keeping Up Appearances' and 'As Time Goes By.' Because he'd seen the first episode, he dozed off. He slept so soundly that he never woke up when the nurse came in to turn off the television.

Early Sunday morning Dr. Duma stuck his head in the doorway to let him know he hadn't forgotten about him. "They're doing a rush job on the tests. We should know the results this afternoon. You've been in good health, haven't you?"

"I guess so."

"Have any mosquitoes bitten you?"

"I don't think so. Gnats on the golf course can be bothersome, but no mosquitoes. Oh, one might have bit me when I turned on the water faucet in the bushes. My hand itched, but I thought it was from the poison oak at the golf course."

"Well, we'll just have to wait for the tests. Try to get a good rest. Do you have any sleeping aids? I'll have the nurse leave you some."

Joe motioned goodbye. "Thanks for dropping in. It's a little too quiet here."

On Sunday afternoon, Anita poked her masked face in the door and told him church members prayed for him during the morning service. "The nurses won't allow me in your room. Bill and Sally, and Katsunaga called. They hope you'll get well soon. They're anxious to talk with you about the presentation. Katsunaga said he's come up with some good material. It's a true love story of great sacrifice. He thinks it's exactly what your speech needs.

"I'd better go. I'll come back tomorrow."

"Dr. Duma expects the test results today."

"Good," she smiled, then threw a kiss at him and eased the door shut.

It's awful to be left behind like this, Joe thought. He felt deserted.

As Joe mulled over his solitary confinement, he heard a knock. The door slowly opened. It was Pastor Blomberg from Grace Alone Church. Even with the mask, he knew his pastor's voice. "I'm not allowed in, but could you manage to come over to the door. I've brought Communion for you. Anita told me you'd appreciate it."

Standing by the partly opened door, Joe reached and took the wafer, then the cup of wine. He knew he no longer stood abandoned. Christ and his church were there with him. Although his legs wobbled, power had been unleashed in his body. In his heart he believed the illness could not last long, no matter what the tests showed. When the nurse took his temperature at 4:00, it had dropped to 99.5.

Later that afternoon, his telephone rang. "This is Dr. Duma. Forgive me for not coming to see you, but I promised my wife and daughter to take them to see 'The Return of the King.' The lab called to tell me that it looks like you have the West Nile virus. Fortunately we've caught it early."

"So, the nurse's hunch was right. But that's strange. I feel better now. My temperature has dropped."

"Huh? That's hard to believe. I expected it to be around 102 or 103 by now."

"I feel much better."

"I'll drop in on you first thing in the morning."

Joe slept soundly that night and was wide awake when Dr. Duma came to the room at 6:30 a.m. "Are you still feeling better?" he asked.

"I feel quite normal, but I've decided not to play golf this morning."

"It's hard to understand. I wouldn't believe it if the tests hadn't been so conclusive. You amaze me, Joe Weaver. You must have a special pipeline to God."

"Not pipeline; we're wireless." Joe smiled at the doctor. "You've seen strange healings before, haven't you? You need to understand, Dr. Duma, that I believe God has given me an important assignment. In cases like this, one can pray with confidence, almost certain — at least as humanly possible — that God will heal, or if not heal, make an alternative way possible. Sounds incredible, doesn't it? But in my heart I've learned to believe it."

"Let's wait a day to see how you do. At this rate you may be able to go home on Tuesday."

40
Surprise Visitor

Tuesday morning, Jay Glenwood, a golf buddy from church, surprised Joe when he opened the door and pushed a wheelchair next to the bed. "Time to get up and get out," he said.

"Didn't you play golf this morning?"

"Sure, but this is my day for volunteering. I push patients around. Your wife is here with the car. She's waiting downstairs. Do you have all your things in that bag? Could you hold it in your lap?"

Joe slid out of bed. Jay offered to help him into the wheelchair, but Joe said, "I'm okay. I can manage."

"Regulations are regulations." Joe pushed Jay's arm aside and sat down under his own power.

"Amazing, how you recovered so fast."

"I'll join you for golf tomorrow," Joe said with an almost believable tone of honesty.

After he was seated in the car and buckled in, Anita reached over to grip his arm and said, "You won't believe what happened last night."

"What?"

"We'll wait till we get home. I don't want you fainting on me."

Joe had never seen his wife so secretive. He felt like forcing her to stop the car and tell him. When they reached their street, he said,

"Don't bother to park by the house. I can walk from the carport. I feel completely normal."

"You must have had only a pollen attack."

"But blood tests don't lie, unless there's been a mistake."

They got out of the car and walked to the house. Joe flaunted his recovery by pumping his tote bag as though marking time to a tune.

Entering the house, Joe clicked on the fan and turned on the air conditioning, then went to the kitchen to brew a pot of coffee.

"So, what's the big news you're holding back?" he asked when he entered the living room.

"Sit down first. I don't want you to collapse from shock."

"Is it that bad?"

"No, no, good! Should I start now, or do we wait for your coffee?" she asked teasingly.

"For goodness sake, out with it."

"Are you all set?" she asked with dramatic seriousness. "When I came home from the hospital yesterday, Sylvia Jansen was waiting for me. She had with her a young woman and her little girl and boy. Guess who *she* was?"

"Get on with the story. Who was it?"

"Are you ready for this? Elna McGibbon. I invited them in. Sylvia has been Elna's friend for quite a while, all the way back from Berkeley days. Elna had come to see Sylvia. While they talked, Sylvia mentioned you and me. Elna had heard something about our acquaintance with Michael, her husband."

"Husband? They're divorced."

"That's what we thought. He'd run off to live with his homosexual partner, but there was no official divorce."

"Well? What did Elna want?"

"Another shocker was that McGibbon's partner left him for another lover."

Joe was about to say, "How ironic!" but pursed his lips and kept quiet.

Sylvia said that she thought Michael wanted to start over with Elna.

"For the kids' sake, I suppose," Joe said.

"That, too, but he seems very remorseful. He realizes what a fool he's been and believes he still loves his wife."

"Then, will he keep fighting for gay rights in the church?"

"Sylvia says he'll keep advocating for GLEE, but may not be as radical as before."

"A wounded healer?" Joe wondered. "He may be a more effective advocate than ever now. What does Sylvia suggest?"

"Nothing for the moment, except pray."

"What's Elna doing in LaVerne?"

"Working in a Christian elementary school. It also has a pre-school program. The two little ones go there."

"Must be tough financially. No alimony if no divorce. How does Elna look?"

"She's from the happy Dane tradition. It's hard to say at first glance, but if I were a man, I think she'd make me very happy."

"She must resemble you then."

"I won't answer that, but I'm sure she's more sexy than any man could be."

That seemed to be the cue for Anita to retreat to her study to play Free Cell on her computer. That was her way of relaxing, emptying her mind of all worries.

The surprising news about Elna McGibbon drove Joe to serious pondering. He didn't know what he should do next. He sat thinking, but it got him nowhere. He circled in his mind, always returning to where he started. If he could only decide his next step .... Suddenly without thinking, he began humming Henry Newman's "Lead Kindly Light." When he came to the last line of stanza one, he sang the words aloud, "one step enough for me." But what was that step? "Lord," he prayed, "show me my next move. No sooner had he asked that when he thought of his companions. *I'll telephone each of them. Try to arrange a meeting.*

"Ani," he called out, "could you come here. I need your help."

"You're not at the computer already?" she shouted back.

"I need your help" was the code phrase for "I've messed up on the computer. Save me!"

She came walking toward his study. "Over here," he said. "I need to call our pastors for a meeting. Could you do that for me? Just the four key ones and Bill and Sally."

"Why not E-mail them and give two or three choices for meeting times?"

"I think we need to get together soon. Ask them for tomorrow, Friday or Saturday morning. Be sure to thank them for their concern about my health. Tell them I'm completely well and that I need their wisdom for Assembly preparations. Ask them to reply as soon as possible."

By 9:00 that night, all had called. Each one independently selected Friday morning. He thought that boded well for the meeting.

41
Bound for Destruction

The night before they gathered, Joe wrestled in bed with himself. He believed in his head that he and his comrades were on the right path, but doubts afflicted his heart. Like a viral infection attacking the soul, his confidence dissipated. Time and again he repeated, "Lord, I believe, help my unbelief." In weariness he finally said to God, "Send your angels to uphold me." He quickly qualified his request. "That would be angels in the form of Wilbur Chan, Isaiah Menkir, Sungdo Kim and Shinichi Katsunaga." As an afterthought, he remembered Sally Ryan and Bill Scully, then his wife lying next to him.

Anita turned over on her right side, facing Joe's back.

"Lord, I must not forget Ani. She's always beside me." When he'd been depressed, she knew how to snap him out of it. Everyone needs a confidant. He recalled Bishop Hans Lilje's admonition to the missionaries in Hiroshima: "Never be a loner; always have someone with whom you can confide." Anita had fulfilled that role, even sometimes becoming a devil's advocate. The older he became, the more he thanked God for his wife. Like an alert lifeguard she had rescued him many times.

With that gracious thought, he slid out of bed and went to the living room. The TV clock said 4:54. Anita's alarm would soon go off, and she'd come for a devotional reading and prayer. It was her turn to pray aloud. As always she'd mention persons he didn't know were sick. These prayers sensitized them to think of others, not just their own problems. The American flag flying outside their window caused them to broaden their prayers to include the President and government officials, and always a word for suffering people in the world, especially those victimized by war. "May good come from all this evil," would close the prayer.

Because of a lingering tiredness from his illness, Joe didn't play golf. He confined his exercise to a few push-ups and some exercises dating back to middle school days when he worked his shoulder muscles to sharpen his pitching curveball.

That brought back memories of his youth and games of long ago. He wondered what curveballs might be thrown at him today. Certainly there would be some surprises. He couldn't predict what his friends would offer up. It promised to be an exciting morning.

As he expected, the Japanese pastor arrived exactly at 9:00, followed by the Korean, Chinese and Ethiopian. Bill and Sally came late, but Joe suggested waiting for them while drinking coffee.

The living room looked crowded with eight people in a circle. The large stylistic black and white painting of Mt. Fuji above the fireplace dominated the room. The north-side windows let in a view of outdoor greenery. On the north wall above the piano, the bluish Sadao Watanabe woodblock print of Jesus in Gethsemane silently witnessed the scene.

Joe Weaver looked around at his colleagues. "Sungdo Kim prayed last time. Sally would you mind doing the honors today?" After that, since the purpose of the meeting was clear, they jumped in with their ideas for the mission rally.

As the leader, Wilbur Chan began with an example of a Tiananmen Square refugee who had been working to heal the suspicions between the Hong Kong churches and the China Christian Council.

Sungdo Kim followed with the story of a brave couple from Seoul who had gone into North Korea to establish links with the house churches.

Bill Scully spoke of his own efforts to befriend gays on campus.

Sally Ryan told of working with Claremont college students to fight racism.

Isaiah Menkir said, "My example is different. I want to tell you about a man named Tumsa, the General Secretary of the Evangelical Church MekaneYesus. When the communists overthrew Emperor Haile Selassie and confiscated Radio Voice of the Gospel, Tumsa stood firm, all 6 feet 6 inches of him, and suffered martyrdom as a result."

"I remember him," Joe said. "I met him at Asmara in the early '70s. No one knew for a long time what happened to him."

Following several moments of quiet, Joe said, "We shouldn't overlook my wife. In the Tokyo telephone counseling service, she had many chances to help couples stay together. But the plight of the gays especially troubled her. We should never minimize their hurts. They had no place to go for help in Japan, especially high schoolers. There were no books available, so they'd call the telephone service.

"What about you, Shinichi?"

"Saa," he grimaced. "Nothing directly that I can think of. But maybe an indirect example would work."

"How do you mean?" Chan asked.

"Take Jesus, for instance. He used parables to sneak up on the audience from the side."

"Do you have an example?"

"I brought along a video based on a true story. It's called '*The Shiokari Pass.*'"

"We used it in a media campaign during the late '70s," Joe said. "But how use it?"

"That could be difficult, but not impossible."

"We're in the dark," Chan said. "Have you got the video? Is it in Japanese or English?"

"It's the English version. Maybe we should view it." Shinichi started the tape and pushed the fast-forward button. "It's a love story about a young Christian railway worker who had waited seven years while his sweetheart recovered from tuberculosis. Finally she became well enough so that the young man and she agreed to marry.

But just before the engagement ceremony…. Oh, here it is." He pushed the play button and they witnessed a dramatic example of self-sacrifice. Although only a brief segment, all of them in the room ended up wiping tears from their eyes.

"Wow!" Bill said. "Powerful stuff! You must work that into your speech."

They sat in silence for a while, then Chan asked, "How could we use it?"

Menkir answered, "Everyone in the film is bound for destruction. Somehow, some way had to be found to prevent it. That young man did it. Can't you see it? It's a perfect metaphor, or parable describing what we in the church must do. Otherwise we split and die; our church withers away."

Joe spoke. "Dr. Henke says we can use visuals and project onto a screen."

"All we need is that two or three minute climax," Menkir said.

Sensing the need for a break, Anita said, "I'll bring the coffee for refills. If you need a washroom, it's the first door on the right."

Joe just had to add, "And I cleaned it nicely for your sakes."

42
A Losing Fight?

While they munched homemade almond bars and drank coffee, Joe thought it would be a good time to report the news on the McGibbons.

"A few days ago an unexpected visitor surprised us. You can't imagine who?" Joe looked to see who would venture a guess.

"McGibbon?" said Sally.

"Close, very close. It was his wife Elna."

"You're kidding," Bill said. "Whatever for?"

"Haven't you been praying for them?" Joe scanned the faces of his guests. "Confess up. Who has prayed for them? Raise your hand." From left to right everyone raised a hand.

"Remarkable!" Joe exclaimed, then caught himself. "When we obey Jesus and pray for our adversaries, why should we be surprised when people actually do?"

Anita had been waiting to speak. "McGibbon had some trouble with his partner. He realizes now how much he misses Elna and the two kids. They were here, too. Two and four-years old."

"Does that mean he won't be pushing the gay agenda anymore?" Wilbur Chan asked.

"Elna thinks he'll continue but won't be quite as strident as before."

"Did you see the morning paper?"Chan asked. "The California Supreme Court annuled the 4,000 same-sex marriages in San Francisco." Chan took the paper from his briefcase and passed it around.

"What happens now to those couples?" Bill asked. "Last week Missouri passed a constitutional amendment banning same-sex marriages. That was their way of blocking judges from approving them."

Menkir spoke next. "It's a very confusing time. God only knows how this will turn out."

"There's another element in this whole debate which we overlook," Joe said. "The other night on TV, the announcer interviewed a Tom Coleman who heads up the Unmarried America movement. He stated that the vast majority of unmarried people in the U.S. are not homosexual. There are 86 million unmarried Americans. They make up 42 percent of the U.S. work force, but it's the gays and lesbians who garner the spotlight and push for same-sex marriage. Most singles, he claims, only want to be treated as individuals having equal status with other citizens."

"I didn't realize that," Bill said. "The gay-rights advocates certainly have taken over the cause."

"Bill Moyer interviewed conservative Cal Thomas on TV," Joe said. "Thomas shocked me when he said the gay and lesbian movement is winning the struggle. Some letters to the editor in the *Chronicle* say the same. They claim the younger generation is much more willing to accept gays and same-sex marriages. It's only a matter of time before they will be in the majority."

"What does that mean for the church?" asked Kim.

Bill Scully reached into his briefcase and pulled out a newspaper clipping. "Did any of you see what Alan Dershowitz said about this? If I understand him correctly, he says the government should stay out of the marriage business, confine itself to civil unions and let the religious bodies do the marriages. He thinks that would strengthen the wall of separation of church and state."

"Who is he?" Katsunaga asked.

"A very famous Harvard law professor."

Joe nodded. "Usually I'm on the opposite side of Dershowitz's arguments, but I think he's on the right track this time."

"You mean, don't let the state use the term *marriage*?" Menkir asked.

"From what I read," Sally said, "the same-sex marriage advocates won't settle for anything less than marriage. They say they'd still be discriminated against."

"We must keep marriage with its traditional meaning as a union of a man and a woman," Menkir insisted. "Otherwise we open the door for polygamy and all its tragic consequences."

"Supposing," Joe began, "we take the Dershowitz argument a step further."

"Good grief!" Anita exploded. "How can you go beyond that?"

"Calm down, dear. Listen, you never listen to me," he smiled. "Surrender even the word *marriage* to civil authorities. They've been called marriage licenses ever since I can remember. Okay? Let couples do marriages however they choose. But we in the church perform only Services of Holy Matrimony, for heterosexual couples. For us it's a Christian service with a wedding involved and sometimes Holy Communion. The church decides its standards. Let the state set its standards."

The pastors' faces looked skeptical. Kim responded first. "But aren't we all citizens, too? I can't imagine my people giving up, surrendering so much to the government — and to homosexuals."

"I see Kim's point," Bill said. "Wouldn't it make us two-faced? We'd be surrendering our civil responsibilities to one set of standards and church responsibilities to another."

Joe could see a puzzled expression on Kim's face, who then said, "That won't be the first time. When I served in the Korean army, I had to do my civil duty, even maybe kill someone." He laughed, then added, "In church I act better."

"So?" Chan interrupted. "At our Southern California Synod Assembly, we gave our approval to GLEE's proposal for blessing same-sex couples and ordaining non-celibate homosexuals."

"But that was only a tactic to get our own motion passed on to the General Assembly," said Menkir shaking his head. "I doubt if we could expect our congregations to go along with us on that. We'd all be fired."

"This is getting heavy. Let's take a five-minute break," Chan proposed. "We need to clear our heads."

43
Doubt

Menkir stepped outside and lit a cigarette. Katsunaga sat by himself. The others moved about, either grabbing a cookie or heading to the washroom. Anita brought in two dishes of mixed nuts and set them on the coffee table. Joe went to the kitchen and prepared another pot of coffee, this time with the carmel-cream blend.

When they returned to their seats, Chan attempted to summarize the issues. He concluded by saying, "The key question is whether or not to repeal the bans on blessing same-sex couples and the ordaining of practicing homosexuals. Let's focus only on those two points, alright?"

Sally raised her hand. "Before we discuss that, may I tell a story that might be helpful?"

"If it's pertinent, go on," Chan said.

"This may sound funny, but it could be meaningful. When I was in high school, my friends and I attended a tabernacle in Los Angeles. I forget the name of the preacher. He had come from Scotland and had a distinct Scottish brogue. I can't imitate him, but I'll try.

"There was this couple getting dressed for church. The wife looked at her husband, who was examining the collar on his white shirt. He held it up to the window for a better look. His wife warned him, 'If it's *dutful*, it's dirty.'"

"What's the point?" Bill asked.

"If we are not absolutely convinced of what we are about to do, we shouldn't do it."

The pastors nodded in agreement.

Sally added, "In America, a suspect in a felony is considered innocent until proved guilty."

"That's apples and oranges," Bill said. "You can't apply criminal law to same-sex matters."

"You listen, Bill. The church regulations now in force must be proved wrong beyond reasonable doubt. Are you willing to say that these pastors could act without any hesitation to upturn the present rules?"

Bill was speechless. Sally looked at the pastors, Anita and Joe. "Are you 100 percent certain that the guidelines should be rescinded? If so, on the basis of what in Scripture?"

"Love." Anita whispered to Sally. "Jesus accepted all people."

"I'm sorry. I thought that story might be helpful."

"The Bible does speak about similar problems," Kim said. "I was reading only last week the passage about eating meat sacrificed to idols. Do you have an English translation here?"

"There's a modern version by my chair," Joe responded. He picked it up and passed it over to Kim, who quickly found the verses and handed the Bible to Bill. "Will you read it to us. Romans 14:21-23.

> "'It is good not to eat meat or drink, wine or do anything that makes your brother or sister stumble. The faith that you have, have as your own conviction before God.
>
> Blessed are those who have no reason to condemn themselves because of what they approve. But those who have doubts are condemned if they eat, because they do not act from faith; for whatever does not proceed from faith is sin.'

"It's not only about what we eat," Kim explained. "It's about our whole life. We must not cause other people to go against their consciences."

"That's only one passage." Anita looked at Kim.

"You can find other places. But that's the clearest."

Chan got up, walked into the dining room and looked out the window. He held up his arms, then turned back to join the others. "I thought we wanted to emphasize reconciliation. How can we put our arguments together so that they make sense?"

Joe hesitated as he waited for others to speak, but then said, "I heard one bishop say, 'This issue can't be resolved; it can only be managed.'"

Katsunaga, who had been staring at the Watanabe woodblock print of Jesus praying in Gethsemane, spoke. "That's our cross. It's a burden too heavy for any of us. Only God in Christ can reconcile us all."

"That's why you showed us that video, isn't it?" Chan asked. "Our dilemmas are too great. Only God is able to deliver us. He dies, that we might be free."

"One of our great Japanese theologians, Kazoh Kitamori, taught us that through God's pain He takes us into himself and gives us the peace beyond understanding."

"That's good!" blurted out Sally.

"We're on the right path now," Chan smiled. "I can feel it. I believe we can help the church get healed in the most basic way."

As Joe looked around the room, he realized that they were experiencing a rare moment of divine insight.

44
Beyond Doubt

The remarkable unanimity of the ethnic pastors produced an inner confidence within Joe. He was certain they could make a convincing case on behalf of the core orthodox tenets of the church. They would base this on the church's central doctrine that God through the cross reconciles them not only to himself but to each other.

During the days that followed, Joe's physical strength increased daily so that by the crucial fourth week of August, he arrived in Minneapolis in full health in spite of the 100-degree heat. The actual site for the General Assembly was to be in Bloomington at a new convention facility near the Mall of America and not far from where the Weavers had lived during a furlough.

Dr. Henke arranged for the Weavers, the four ethnic pastors, Bill Scully and Sally Ryan to stay in a nearby motel in Richfield. On the afternoon of their arrival, Wilbur Chan, Shinichi Katsunaga and Joe visited the convention site to work out the details for the showing of the 3-minute video segment. They were concerned that it pack the most powerful punch possible. It needed to be shown right on cue, with the proper focus and sound.

After Joe returned to the motel, Dr. Henke called. "You arrived safely," he said. "I wanted to make sure you go to the hall to meet with the technicians before tomorrow."

"We've just come from there. They seem to know their stuff, so that's a big relief."

"There's one other matter I need to tell you about, in fact two matters," Henke said.

"Oh! What are they?"

"I'm not sure how to begin." Uncertainty in Henke's voice sent a shiver down Joe's spine. He never liked surprises. He doubted if he could handle any big problem on the eve of the rally.

"Today the Church Council met and Presiding Bishop Frick asked me to attend. They wanted my advice on two related matters, but I didn't know how to respond."

"It's not like you, Dr. Henke. How can I help?"

"The church has received an invitation to send representatives to a peace conference next July in Bethlehem."

"The Holy Land?"

"Yes, there's a very active peace ministry headed by a Palestinian pastor."

"That's good isn't it?"

"Then a few days ago the church received an invitation from the Lutheran churches in Japan to come for a peace conference in Hiroshima, at the time of the 60th anniversary of the atomic bombing, August 6-9."

"So?"

"You were there two months ago. What can you tell me about it?"

He hesitated before answering. "The church itself is beautiful and seats about 500 people. At the entrance you see the image of the Good Shepherd and an inscription saying, 'My house shall be a house of prayer for all nations.' But what do *you* think, Dr. Henke?"

"I can't say anything negative about Bethlehem, except security. The Church Council raised that problem, too."

"The planning committee in Japan, I was told, expects observers from the Catholic, Orthodox and Protestant churches. There will be plenty of press coverage. I'm partial to Hiroshima. I can unequivocally recommend it."

Anita, who had been overhearing the conversation, spoke up. "Joe, stop and think. Aren't you acting on your own? Shouldn't you talk with the pastors before you give advice like that?"

"Dr. Henke, wait a second. My wife is trying to tell me something." He turned to reiterate what Anita had said, then asked her, "Is that right?"

She nodded in agreement.

"Dr. Henke, she thinks we should not act unilaterally but involve our ethnic colleagues."

"The Church Council meets at 8:30 tomorrow morning. They want my opinion by then."

Neither spoke. It was an embarrassingly long silence for Joe. "Could we all meet with you for breakfast?" he finally asked.

Henke, who had worked with former Batak headhunters in Sumatra, got Joe's point at once. "You're right. Anything we suggest should have the backing of the non-Anglos." He paused a moment. "Invite Bill Scully and Sally Ryan. It should be a real education for them."

"Another idea struck me," Joe said. "Who heads up the Doctrinal Adjudication Committee? If we could get him or her to meet with us, wouldn't that help?"

"William Barnett, a professor of dogmatics, is chairperson. I'll try to get a hold of him. When and where should we meet? I'm thinking 6:30 is none too early."

"I thought I saw an IHOP restaurant across from the parking lot. How would that be?"

"Sounds good. I'll try to reserve a corner for eight people. We've got to get this straightened out before the business sessions begin."

45
Bethlehem or Hiroshima

The next day, Joe and Anita awoke early and arrived at IHOP before 6:15. They were ushered to a corner alcove, where ten chairs surrounded a table, resembling a Chinese eating arrangement.

"This is perfect," he said to the waitress.

Because of the seriousness of the meeting, no one arrived late. Dr. Henke asked each pastor to give his name and church, but he introduced Dr. Barnett. To speed up ordering he passed around a paper where they could write their name and the number of the breakfast combination they wanted.

While the list circulated, Henke opened the discussion. "Concordia has received two invitations to send representatives next summer to peace conferences, one at Bethlehem and the other in Hiroshima. The Church Council originally leaned toward the Holy Land, but uncertainty over visas and security caused them to hesitate. Then a few weeks ago the Lutheran churches in Japan sent an invitation for Hiroshima. That would coincide with the observance of the 60th anniversary of the first A-bomb. The Council members are unsure of how to respond. They felt your advice would be valuable in helping them decide which invitation to accept."

No one appeared ready to speak. Henke turned to Joe. "You visited there two months ago. What were your impressions?"

"Anita and I are hardly impartial judges. We worked there after the War. We would love to see the CLC recommend Hiroshima. The new church is magnificent and artistically conducive for discussing peace and justice. It seats 500 and is located on *Heiwa* Boulevard, which leads to the A-bomb Museum."

Anita broke in, "And the new bullet train called *Nozomi* means hope. It makes it from Tokyo to Hiroshima in only six hours."

Isaiah Menkir raised his hand. "In church history, Jesusalem played a central role. The first major church conference was held there. That's when the issues were decided about how many of the Jewish customs were necessary for Gentile Christians to observe. In the light of the present divisive debate over homosexuality, Jerusalem would serve as an ideal location, if it weren't for the security issue. Also, homosexuality is very sensitive for Muslims. To discuss that openly in the Middle East could be explosive."

Sungdo Kim spoke next. "While America fights in Iraq and Afghanistan to bring them liberty, it would be educational for people to see how democracy is doing in Japan and Korea, not perfect but functioning."

Dr. Barnett asked about visas for visitors.

"No problem," Joe replied. "And Japan has one of the lowest crime rates in the world."

Turning to Wilbur Chan, Henke asked, "You haven't said anything?"

He responded quickly. "Any efforts to promote understanding is good. We in Hong Kong successfully hosted the 1997 Assembly of the Lutheran World Federation. That boosted good relations between China and Japan. We'd welcome the conference in our part of the world."

"Pastor Katsunaga, you haven't said anything yet? What do you think?"

"Tell them about your grandfather who worked with us," Joe urged. "About his turn around."

"Do we have time?" he asked.

The others nodded consent, so he told the story. "My grandfather was part of Japan's last hope to defeat America. The military desperately wanted to prevent the invasion of Okinawa and the homeland. People were prepared to fight even with bamboo sticks if the Emperor ordered it."

Shinichi looked down at his hands. He gripped them tight, then took out his handkerchief and wiped his forehead. "The navy forced my grandpa to pilot a one-man torpedo submarine to attack U.S. warships. He failed and drifted several days at sea."

Noticing that Shinichi had choked up, Anita finished the account. "His grandfather opened a can of beans with his teeth. Can you imagine that? Otherwise he never would have survived." Regaining his composure, Shinichi raised his voice. "We Japanese committed ourselves to peace and the peace Constitution. Our church people would make the conference a success. On the sexuality issue, you won't get any trouble from Muslims. We have very few of them."

Looking around the table, Dr. Henke asked, "Does anyone object to our encouraging the Church Council to vote for Hiroshima?" No one responded.

"Thanks for your help. I'll present your consensus to the Church Council. Thanks for your wisdom."

46
The Battle Begins

As the Weavers walked across the parking lot with Dr. Barnett, they saw a long line of pickets. The demonstrators carried professionally-produced signs and banners and a few crude amateur ones. They proclaimed equal rights for gays and lesbians.

Equality now!

Justice for all!

If baptized, why not ordained?

WWJD — What Would Jesus Do?

Men Divide; God Unites.

Be 21st Century Disciples

A baton-waving woman led the marchers chanting, "One, two, three, who are we? People free; free for Thee."

They marched in time to the beat, but few could stay in step for long.

"Round and round we go, the walls of Concordia down must go."

Instead of circling back to the main entrance, the marchers kept going.

"They're imitating Joshua's army, tramping around the convention center like the Israelites at the Battle of Jericho," Joe blurted.

"They make quite a picture," said Anita. "Why didn't you bring the camera, Joe? They're mostly young people and a few clergy."

"I hope they stay peaceful," Barnett said.

"I don't recognize any Lutheran ministers," Henke said. "Other churches must have sent supporters."

Joe broke into a grin. "Do you think the walls will stand up?"

"I don't think these people are joking," Barnett responded. "How long will it take them to circle the building?"

"At least half an hour," Henke guessed. "The newspapers will get plenty of photos."

As Henke and company entered the building, ushers handed them the program for opening worship. Presiding Bishop Alfred Frick was listed as preacher.

"Delegates, please pick up your materials over at the right, observers move to the left," a recorded message announced.

"I guess here's where we separate. Ani, maybe you can sit with Bill and Sally." Joe walked over to the far right and picked up his packet under the W sign. Behind the table about 10-feet high, a TV screen monitored the Assembly hall. Since it was early, few delegates had taken their seats, so Joe decided to browse among the book tables.

The first display featured *Christian Sexuality*, edited by Russell E. Saltzman and a set of Cassette tapes and CDs on *Sex and Sanctity: Robert Gagnon on Homosexuality and the Bible*. Joe thumbed through the book and recognized some of the essayists. Gagnon had done one of the chapters. Joe was tempted to purchase the book, but realized it was too late to add anymore information to the presentation.

He checked out the displays for Lutheran Social Services and Minnesota Lutheran Homes, as well as other special ministries. When he noticed delegates scurrying toward the hall, he realized he'd better find his seat. As he backtracked by the registration table, he bumped into Dr. Henke.

"How'd your meeting go?"

"Fine, they unanimously recommended Hiroshima. Thanks for your help. Now we hope the Assembly will approve."

Joe's assigned seat was toward the back. Water bottles and paper cups occupied the middle of the table. Right after Joe sat down, Pastor Katsunaga appeared.

"We're assigned to the same table," he said as took the seat next to Joe.

Joe presumed that Dr. Henke had arranged for the two of them to sit together. "By the looks of the agenda, we won't get into tough matters until tomorrow. That's good. Tonight we'll try to lay the groundwork."

Wilbur Chan and Isaiah Menkir found their way to the table. "Any news?" Chan asked.

"The Council endorsed Japan for the peace conference."

"Good, now if you can inspire the audience tonight, maybe we can do some healing for the church."

"Did you see the gays and lesbians parading outside?" Menkir asked. "They've gone around the building twice already. A sound truck out there is playing 'Joshua at the Battle of Jericho' over and over again."

"I was surprised," Chan said, "that someone has put the question about blessing same-sex couples and ordaining non-celibate homosexuals on the schedule for later today. How did they manage to move that up?"

"It's McGibbon's payback time. We must get that changed, otherwise my appeal will come too late."

Chan nodded. Menkir then spoke. "Let's put up a counterproposal."

47
Ahead of the Curve

"Here it comes," Joe predicted to Shinichi.

The Church Secretary went to the microphone. "The next item on the agenda is a resolution from the Gay and Lesbians for Evangelical Equality. This recommendation has been forwarded to the General Assembly from the Southern California Synod. It is presented after inconclusive deliberations in the Church Council of Bishops. It reads as follows:

> PREAMBLE. American society is passing through a seismic shift in values. This has been caused by scientific advances which affirm that a human's sexual orientation is established at the moment of conception. With rare exceptions a person with homosexual orientation cannot be changed to heterosexual. The American Psychiatric Association has endorsed this fact. To seek to alter a person's sexual orientation can undermine the individual's self-esteem and personhood.
>
> To deprive homosexuals of equal treatment under the law violates their civil rights and should be condemned. We must treat them no differently than heterosexuals. We advocate that the laws of the United States and the Church must be amended to ensure equal treatment for all citizens and church members.

Our Concordia Lutheran Church, USA should not lag behind what the states already are beginning to do. We need to stay ahead of the curve on this issue and act at this General Assembly to permit the blessing or marriage of same-sex couples. If we approve that, then we logically should rescind the ban on ordaining non-celibate homosexuals; thus we would stand at the forefront of social progress.

The Secretary added, "Because this resolution comes from an association of CLC delegates, there is no need for a second."

By the time the Secretary finished, Wilbur Chan had taken the microphone in the center aisle. He shouted out even before Bishop Frick recognized him. "Mr. Moderator, Bishop Frick. Mr. Moderator, Bishop Frick." Before the noise subsided, Chan declared: "I move that because the GLEE motion has the potential for dividing our Church, we delay debate until tomorrow."

"I second that," a voice sounding like Dr. Henke's resounded loudly.

"May I claim special privilege," Bishop Frick announced, "and commend Pastor Chan and Dr. Henke on this. We need time to sleep on it and pray about it. Shall we say we'll take up the matter after the morning recess tomorrow?" Without calling for a vote, he announced, "We're adjourned for the day."

Joe looked around at the delegates' faces. Some were relieved; others agitated. From outside he could hear the marchers singing the old civil rights refrain, "We Shall Overcome." Then, the sound truck turned up the volume on "Joshua at the Battle of Jericho." The demonstrators had gone around seven times, but the wall still stood.

Joe and Shinichi headed for the lobby to join Anita, Sally and Bill. Intense delegates milled around. The Church was on a collision course with the gay and lesbian locomotive. Chan and Henke had slowed them down for the moment, but who could predict what would happen in the morning?

They joined up with the other three. "We need to talk," Joe said.

The noise in the lobby and the music blaring in from the parking lot forced them to head for the far end of the building where they found a secluded room. They shut the door and sat huddled in one corner.

After a few reactions to the afternoon developments, Joe rose. "Tonight is our night. We must not fail. Emotions run high, at fever pitch. If ever we need to pray, the time is now."

At first Joe started to pray aloud, but stopped. "This time I am standing in the need of prayer. Would someone else pray? Ani, I think it's your turn."

"Me? Why me?"

"Because, I need your prayer, and you're the oldest, besides me. I'm not joking."

"All right, but short is better than long. Help us Lord. Keep us from pride and self-will. Make us do what is right. Use the mission rally to heal our divisions. Make people focus on Jesus. Enable Joe and Katsunaga to speak for you tonight. Assist the technicians, too, and all of us. Accomplish what we cannot do by our own wisdom and strength. 'Our Father, who art in heaven.'" They all stood and prayed together the Lord's Prayer.

As they began to leave the room, Joe said in a barely audible voice, "Thank you all, each of you. May God's will be done."

He then noticed that Shinichi Katsunaga stood waiting in the hall. When Sally Ryan and Bill Scully came out, he stopped them. Not intentionally eavesdropping, Joe couldn't help but hear what Shinichi asked them.

"That story you told about the Scotsman and the dirty collar, were you telling us never to do what we feel is doubtful? That idea troubles me."

"In what way?" Bill asked.

"Suppose we aren't sure of what we're doing at this Assembly."

"For instance? What could we be doing that can be called *dutful*?" questioned Sally.

"It's just a thought, but have we checked on the video we're showing tonight? Do we have permission to show it in public? Pastor Weaver said they had used it publicly in Japan. They had the okay to do that, but what about us thirty years later in America?"

"What are you trying to say?"

"I get it," Sally said. "If we have any doubt about the legality of showing it, we shouldn't do it. Remember what Mrs. Weaver prayed? 'Make us do what is right.'"

Joe stepped closer to them. "If it's doubtful, we must not show it. But my speech depends on that film."

48
The Rally

"Everything is ready," Dr. Henke said to Joe during the organ prelude. "I'm counting on you. God is counting on you." He took hold of Joe's hands, held them tightly, then pushed Joe ahead of him toward the stage. They ascended the stairs to the tune of "We've a Story to Tell to the Nations." Childhood memories of that hymn rushed through Joe's veins, exciting in him the instincts of an apostle.

Level-headed Dr. Henke led the service. Joe could think only about the words he was called to deliver. Suddenly panic attacked him. Speeches delivered long ago reminded him of humiliating memory blocks.

After the hymns and Scripture readings, Henke turned and looked at Joe Weaver sitting to the side of the pulpit, head down between his knees. When Henke spoke his name, he jerked up with a distant stare in his eyes. He slowly stood up, shook Henke's hand and stepped into the pulpit. Gazing out over the hall, he searched for familiar faces. His wife waved at him from the back and pointed upward.

"Yes," he whispered. "You, God, must take charge. Speak the word of peace through me."

Fingering the microphone, he tapped it to be sure his voice would carry. "Dear friends, I know many of you are disappointed that our beloved Dr. Ambrose Kim does not stand here tonight. Instead you have me, an 80-year-old refugee from the post-World War missionary invasion of Japan. We went to our former enemies as messengers of reconciliation. How well we succeeded, only future generations will determine. We can take small credit for Japan's transformation into a peace-loving nation and one of America's truest allies. Oh, we and others bungled many things, but no one can accuse us of not giving our utmost.

"Now by the strangest of circumstances, Dr. Henke has called on me to address you on 'Bridging the Chasm.' As we spanned the gulf between enemies who suffered the attack on Pearl Harbor and the nuclear bombings of Hiroshima and Nagasaki, now we as an American church face an abyss into which we must not fall. Our beloved Concordia Lutheran Church must not split. If we are to keep any credibility in the world, we must not divide over sexuality. That would shame us. Our forefathers and mothers would look down on us, disgraced that they had given birth to us.

"As we heard in the Scripture lesson in Acts 15, the Christian church was on the verge of schism. St. Paul and the Gentile converts in the Roman Empire feared they might be cut off from St. James and the Jewish believers in Jerusalem. Paul and Barnabas traveled back to Jerusalem to seek a solution from James, the head of the Jewish Christians who still followed many of the practices handed down from the ancestors. By facing their differences under the guidance of God's Spirit, they reached a mutually satisfactory understanding.

"James summarized their consensus like this: 'I have reached the decision that we should not trouble those Gentiles who are turning to God, but we should write to them to abstain only from things polluted by idols and from fornication and from whatever has been strangled and from blood. For in every city, for generations past, Moses has had those who proclaim him, for he has been read aloud every sabbath in the synagogues.'

"For you and me at this General Assembly we face the imminent threat of schism. Some of our fellow Christian denominations are in the process of irreparable conflicts. In Christ's name, we must call a halt to divisiveness among us. We must remain one in the Spirit founded upon the Scriptures and our tradition, focused on Jesus, our Lord and Savior.

"As Dietrich Bonhoeffer wrote in *Life Together*, we are called to die, to be crucified with Christ so that the life of Jesus may live in us.

"Our present situation reminds me of two runaway trains, speeding on a collision course. Such a dangerous time calls us to desperate action. My Japanese colleague, Pastor Shinichi Katsunaga, told me he worried about our Church. When I asked him if he knew of any example I could share with you about someone's sacrifice to save a whole community, he gave me a video about a real event that happened in Hokkaido, Japan, a hundred years ago. It tells of a young Christian railway worker on the day of his engagement to his sweetheart who had recovered from seven years of tuberculosis.

"This thirty-year-old man, Nobuo Nagano, is riding a train on his way to the long-awaited engagement ceremony. At this point, I had planned to show you the film version of what occured. But because we failed to get copyright clearance for showing it, you will have to stretch your imaginations like we used to do when listening to the radio. Think of it as a radio drama.

"Are you ready? Here we go.

"The lights dim. Above the altar a huge screen of our imagination descends, and the convention hall reverberates with the rumbling of a steam-powered train lumbering over the rails. We see the train, puff by puff, struggling upward to reach the summit. It creeps through the pass called *Shiokari*. Black clouds of smoke contrast with the white drifts of snow banked beside the rails.

"Inside the rail coach, we see Nobuo Nagano elated over his coming betrothal.

"The train jolts. We hear metal scraping against metal. The dissonant sound alerts Nagano. The car moves out of character. Something is wrong.

"As the coach rounds a curve, a passenger shouts, 'There's no engine behind us!'

"Vibrations from the front engine stop. The train halts abruptly, then begins to move backwards. The scenery they had just passed goes by them.

"Save us, save us! The coupling is broken," a man screams.

"Panic breaks out. "Amida Buddha! Amida Buddha!" a woman shouts.

"Nagano prays. 'Lord Jesus, help me.' He jumps up. 'Be calm. I'll stop it.' He rushes down the aisle to the back platform and grabs the icy brake wheel. He twists with all his might. The car slows. For a moment he thinks they're saved. Relief spreads across the passengers' faces.

But the brake wheel sticks; it will not budge.

"Fifty yards ahead he sees a steep curve. Unless he can prevent the car from moving, it will derail and tumble down a precipice.

"Only one action can save them. Nagano chooses that instinctively, obeying the words he had read the night before. "By this we know love, that he laid down his life for us. And we ought to lay down our lives for the brethren." (I John 3:16)

"Nagano leaps off the rear of the coach, falling onto the rails he wedges his body against the wheels. The car slowly rolls onto his body and stops.

"The screen goes blank. The hall remains dark for what seems like eternity. Then a spotlight shines on Joe Weaver. He waits and waits, then speaks.

"I submit to you that all of us partisans here tonight are aboard separate cars. We are speeding out of control on a collision course. The normal rational brakes don't work. The only way to stop the crash which will destroy our Church is for us to lay down on the tracks. Give our lives that the Church may live. We must crucify ourselves and our agendas that we all may rise to new life.

"Our task tonight is to ask God how we are to die for Christ's sake and the Church's. May we do so in our hearts and rest in peace until tomorrow. Amen.

"Let us close with a favorite hymn of mine: 'Must Jesus Bear the Cross Alone.'"

49
Over the Chasm

The following morning after the break, delegates appeared tense as they returned to their seats. Bishop Frick pounded his gavel. "Will the delegates take their seats. Observers, please stay in your assigned places. Can we have it quiet? Quiet please! The Secretary will read the resolution." He reads it very speedily.

"Mr. Moderator, I rise to a point of order." Isaiah Menkir stood in the center aisle. "The resolution as it reads violates this Church's Constitution." A stunning silence swept over the hall.

"The Constitution says, 'Our congregations accept the canonical Scriptures of the Old and New Testaments as the inspired Word of God and the authoritative source and norm of its proclamation, faith and life.' This has been spelled out in the *Formula of Concord*, which defines what all Lutheran churches in the world accept as authority. To act contrary to our fundamental tenets will remove us from our confessional family in the world.

"We must not repeat the foolish, illegal actions of the mayor in San Francisco. In defiance of the laws of California, he issued marriage licenses to 4,000 same-sex couples. Now the California Supreme Court has declared him out of order, annuling the marriages. We should not repeat such a reckless mistake by defying our own Church Constitution. If we bless same-sex couples and ordain practicing homosexuals, we shall deny the basic Biblical teachings of our Church. Therefore, Mr. Moderator, I make a substitute motion to refer the legitimacy of the resolution to the Doctrinal Adjudication Committee."

"Is there a second?"

The sound of "Second" came from all directions in the hall.

Bishop Frick waited before calling for the vote. "What do the framers of the original resolution have to say about this?"

Who should stand up to answer but Dr. Michael McGibbon?

"Yes, Dr. McGibbon, what can you say?"

"Frankly, sir, I am shocked. After more than eight decades of the CLC's existence, is not this the first time anyone has referred to that doctrinal basis of our Church. These past years have brought to light many enlightening facts about the Bible that shed doubt on traditional interpretations. To be honest, not many of us can unequivocally endorse the wording in the Constitution."

"Am I to take that to mean," Bishop Frick asked, "that you would see value in asking the Doctrinal Adjudication Committee to study this?"

McGibbon delayed before he answered. "Yes, I suppose you could say that."

Wilbur Chan had been waving his hand over at the microphone in the right aisle.

Bishop Frick recognized him. "Yes, Pastor Chan, you have the floor."

"This issue is not only ethical and doctrinal. The implications go well beyond our own CLC in the United States. It is a catholic problem, universal and applicable to all cultures in the world. We in America must not act unilaterally. We need to listen to our sister Lutheran churches, and the other churches, Catholic and Protestant. If we disregard others, many of us could be forced to vote for changes that we have doubts about."

Bishop Frick held up his hand to stop Chan. "You are jumping the gun. Hold your comments until we have heard the invitation to the Hiroshima Peace Conference."

"Sorry, sir, I was out of order."

"Shall we then vote on the substitute motion?"

No one took to the microphones. Joe guessed their lack of response wasn't because they had no opinion, but they'd rather have a committee deal with it out of the public eye. The vote went unanimously in favor of Menkir's substitute to refer it to the Committee.

"Pastor Chan, now we can take up your concern. I'll ask the Secretary to read the invitation from the Lutheran churches of Japan." The Secretary proceeded to read it.

Bishop Frick then posed a question. "Dr. Henke, are you here? Are we to understand that as part of the Peace Conference one whole day will be devoted to sexuality issues?"

"That's correct."

"I see no hands. Are you ready to vote. All in favor, please stand."

To Joe it appeared that everyone had stood, even McGibbon and his comrades around him. In that brief moment of standing, Joe Weaver knew that the opposing sides would become reconciled. The Church would not split. The word of the cross prevailed. God had enabled them to bridge the chasm.

About the Author

He is a native of Gary, Indiana and now resides with his wife Miriam at Pilgrim Place in Claremont, California.

In 2001 he published his first novel, *Pre-emptive Love*, followed by *Golfing in Jesus' Spirit*, both available from Authorhouse at 1-888-280-7715. In *SEXUAL DIVIDE* he tackles the church's struggle over how to deal with homosexuality.

Olson's career included working as a missionary in Hiroshima, Japan and then serving the church's mass media ministry through the Lutheran World Federation Broadcasting Service's Tokyo office. Ecumenically he coordinated Television Awareness Training in Asia, edited the *Japan Christian* Quarterly and helped found the Chinese media ministry of Kairos Communication Service International based in Alhambra, California. In 1982 the Alumni Association of Augustana College (Rock Island, Illinois) bestowed on him the Outstanding Service Award.